DEVELOPING STORY IDEAS

DEVELOPING STORY IDEAS

Michael Rabiger

Focal Press

Boston Oxford Auckland Johannesburg Melbourne New Delhi

This book is printed on acid-free paper.

Library of Congress Cataloging-in-Publication Data

Rabiger, Michael.
    Developing story ideas / Michael Rabiger.
        p.   cm.
    Includes bibliographical references and index.
    ISBN 0-240-80398-1 (pbk : alk. paper)
    1.   Motion picture authorship. I. Title.
PN1996.R16 2000
    808.2'3—dc21   99-055120

British Library Cataloguing-in-Publication Data
A catalogue record for this book is available from the British Library.

The publisher offers special discounts on bulk orders of this book.
For information, please contact:
Manager of Special Sales
Elsevier Science
200 Wheeler Road
Burlington, MA 01803
Tel: 781-313-4700
Fax: 781-313-4802

For information on all Focal Press publications available, contact our World Wide Web homepage at http://www.focalpress.com

10 9 8 7 6 5 4
Printed in the United States of America

In fond memory of Lois Deacon, who said,
"Nothing is real until I have written about it."

Contents

Introduction

Anyone wanting to develop a range of narrative ideas, whether beginner or mature professional, can expect to find the work in this book both exciting and liberating. Although the assignments are aimed primarily at producing work for the fiction and documentary screen, all of them concern core ideas and are handled in outline form. They can just as well seed work in other media such as theater, radio, journalism, prose fiction or even conceivably dance.

This book was written to answer a pressing need for screen works with more individuality, focus, and personal voice. Aspiring screenwriters and directors nowadays begin their profession not by professional apprenticeship but in film schools. During their relatively short existence, most such schools have been preoccupied with teaching production techniques. Now that this goal is largely accomplished, most find their students producing well-made films that are alarmingly unoriginal in content and message. In my experience, film students around the world present a surprisingly uniform and limited range of ideas. This could be due to the global TV culture that has colonized the world's living rooms. By age eighteen the average person is said to have seen eighteen thousand hours of television. Everywhere people seem to wear the same clothes, eat the same food, watch the same movies, and get the same news and information. It's hardly surprising, therefore, if ideas for film projects lack individuality.

To the ubiquity of TV culture, add the fact that the average person gets an average education. This stresses memory and mental agility, discounts the individual's inner, emotional self, and encourages students to see other people as competitors. Such indoctrination is disabling for work in the arts, especially in such collaborative disciplines as film, theater, and dance. To grow—in life and in making art—one must take emotional risks, create actively and repeatedly, and create *with* other people, not in rivalry with them.

The work in this book aims to return you to the unique value of your own experience. You may be a student, or you may be halfway through life and looking for renewal in your writing. The work begins by helping you reflect on how your life has marked you, and it then leads you through the artistic process. It lays out a path to create collaboratively, take emotional risks, and profit from a spectrum of stimulating resources. It teaches the elements of dramaturgy painlessly and practically, through discussing the examples of the writing required by the assignments. By the end, you should be able to generate a wide variety of personally felt stories without having to imitate or to wait for inspiration.

Although this book will often be used in group settings, it can also greatly benefit those working alone who are looking for methods that lead to visual, behavioral plots. If you are using this book alone, expect:

- An approach that leads just as well toward other narrative forms, like radio, journalism, television, literary fiction, and theater.
- Work appropriate to beginners or to more advanced writers, to under-graduates, graduates, experienced or inexperienced writers, old or young—anyone wanting to create more and better stories.
- Preliminary exercises to help you form a working notion of your artistic identity.
- Short writing assignments that concentrate on essence, not on length, bulk, or polished form.
- A spectrum of personal and communal resources that any writer can use.
- Clear and simple definitions of dramaturgical tools and terminology.
- Writing samples with an accompanying critique that shows the tools of dramatic analysis at work.
- An evenhanded approach to fiction and nonfiction, one that assumes the value of each form and their presence in each other.
- An emphasis on narrative through image and action rather than spoken language.
- Nonfiction treated as fiction's equal, not a poor relation.

If you are using this book in a class or writers' self-help group, you should in addition expect:

- Your teacher or group leader to use the book flexibly, adapting it to personal preferences and experience.
- To get valuable experience from presenting your ideas to audiences of peers.
- To give and receive critiques in class.
- To find yourself be in a learning community, one where theory, practice, and critique are intertwined and practiced in an atmosphere of intensity and sharing.

- To get to know others in the group unusually well and to become known and valued by them.
- To find future work partners.

Naturally, no writing course can right the wrongs of contemporary schooling or reverse the assault of corporately controlled mass culture, but the work and its methods can point in the right direction. The assignments constantly integrate practice, theory, and discussion so that each illuminates, refreshes, and reinforces the worth of the other. Most significantly, they lead you to look inward and draw an artistic self-profile. This helps frame your "unfinished business"—the sublimated personal agenda that everyone must pursue in daily living if they are to be truly alive.

Through experience at hands-on projects, an emphasis on self-actualization, and working as part of a learning community, you can expect to form the kinds of creative partnerships that make filmmaking (and just about everything else) so gratifying and productive. This is learning by doing.

The last parts of this book contain brief guidance for those turning an outline into a full screenplay or other dramatic work. There you will find options for developing a dramatic structure, and a host of guidelines to help develop crisp, individual dialogue and active characters. There are specialized bibliographies after most sections, as well as a chapter of detailed help for teachers and group leaders who are new to teaching ideation.

Many people contributed to this book. At New York University, I am indebted to the film department faculty for their discussions and friendship, in particular Lora Hays, George Stoney, Ken Dancyger, Marketa Kimbrell, and Nick Tanis. I must also thank Dean Mary Schmidt Campbell, who kindly invited me to NYU for a wonderful year of teaching.

I owe much gratitude to my NYU students, who generously permitted me to reproduce their writing. Their hard work and infectious enthusiasm made our classes a joy to teach, and without them there would literally be no book. They came from France, Korea, Norway, Mexico, Britain, Canada, and of course the United States. Thank you Michelle Arnove, Bryan Beasley, Leah Cho, Chris Darnley, Paul Flanagan, Angela Galean, Michael Hanttula, Margaret Harris, Kundong Lee, Louis Leterrier, Amanda McCormick, Alex Meilleur, Cynthia Merwath, Tatsuyo Ohno, Joy Park, Trish Rosen, Peter Riley, Vilka Tzouras, Sharmaine Webb, and Julie Werenskiold. Each piece of writing bears its author's name; if you are in a position to hire their talents, please write me via the publisher, and I will gladly relay inquiries.

At Focal Press, my thanks go to Marie Lee and Karen Speerstra for their long-term support and encouragement. I am especially grateful to my esteemed and overworked colleagues Doreen Bartoni, Cari Callis, and Joe Steiff at my home institution of Columbia College. They critiqued the entire manuscript and contributed a wealth of ideas and corrections. With so much help, all remaining errors in this book are truly my own.

My toughest critic is my wife Nancy Mattei. To her, heartfelt appreciation for her contributions and for putting up with the antisocial habits that I attribute to writing.

Michael Rabiger
Chicago, 2000

PART I

OVERVIEW

1

This Book and Its Goals

THE WORK

Though aimed primarily at those writing for the screen, this book's methods can just as well lead to short stories, a novel, or a play. The skills you will be developing while doing this work are already in great demand, and they will become more so. With fiber cable and satellite access reaching into every home, there is a growing hunger for original story material and good narrative skills. Such forms as fiction, history, documentary, animation, and educational, game, and interactive media all stand or fall on the ability to tell a good story. Even Hollywood, bombarded by thousands of scripts weekly, complains incessantly of a shortage of material that is fresh in voice, vision, and point of view.

Many people who like writing feel inadequate when it comes to finding story ideas and designing plots or story structures. Young (and not so young) writers often feel that nothing has really ever happened to them. They compensate by working from the outside inward, emulating types of stories, or writers that they admire. Like actors trying to learn from other actors, this neglects their most precious resource—what the writer has seen and experienced. By the age of twenty or earlier, everyone has seen some version of everything that life has to offer. Analogously, one has experienced victory, love, overthrow, ejection from Eden, death—everything.

The fatal impediment is not lack of experience but lack of knowing how to recognize, value, and shape it. The key lies in what Thomas Hardy called "moments of vision," those instants of piercing clarity when one stumbles on a special truth or meaning. Everyone carries a stock of such moments and keeps experiencing more of them. So if you are willing to work at writing, you already have the key to producing a flow of moving and effective stories. Priming the pump is this book's purpose.

Of course, many screenwriting manuals exist to do this, but they never seem to discuss how to generate a range of ideas or how to test each idea's strength and meaning. Instead, most presume that you want to become a Hollywood writer, intent on shaping products especially for the American TV networks or studios. But most writers want to develop something that reflects themselves and their own reality, not the preferences of a market or industry.

To be original, writers, composers, and other artists must be able to think radically at the outset. For after the basics are laid down and elaboration is under way, it is difficult or impossible to make a cliched idea into something better. This is like trying to redesign the steelwork in a finished skyscraper. One *must* get the foundation right from the first; examining narrative ideas and experimenting at the ideation stage are the ways to do this.

Since designing such fundamentals is demanding, it's a stage that is fatally easy to leapfrog—hence the focus of this book on writing in outline form. This keeps your basic ideas compact and highly visible. Because you and your critical readers can see the fundamentals of your story's characters, dynamics, balance, and meaning, you can easily make changes. This is much harder once you have invested a lot of work in writing an elaborate screenplay; by then, one is naturally more resistant to changes, especially as one cannot see the woods for the trees.

Writing in outline also helps you to create stories as if you were an observer seeing from the outside, which is vital in screenplay work. Many people habitually write from inside the main character looking out. But a camera and sound recorder are like eyes and ears that look on from the outside and can only see verbal or physical actions; they cannot enter anyone's psyche or film thoughts and feelings.

In this, the cinema is like life itself. We figure out another person's inner feelings and motivations from observing what he does. We never enter his mind. Only in literature is this possible. Working in outline, therefore, helps to produce writing that can be filmed, but it also produces the basis for an observational literary style, if that is your aim.

Through games and self-examination exercises, you will see what acute observation and playful improvisation can do for a writer. You will learn how the artistic process works through doing it, and you will uncover your underlying interests and artistic identity through self-analysis exercises.

The writing assignments use uncomplicated methods, and they connect you with a spectrum of resources. Even for the adaptation and documentary work, the assignments should help you reach for original ideas and approaches. Most chapters have a short bibliography, if you want information in greater depth.

Because the major elements of each story are so accessible, they can be presented to the group for reaction and critique. From this the writer gets an early and vital experience with an audience. This, surely the object and final gratification of all artistic work, is normally withheld from the screenwriter for an unconscionably long time.

From classroom sessions of dramatic analysis that others apply to your work and that you apply to theirs, you will learn how to break stories into their working parts and how to reassemble them, perhaps differently. This helps one dig deeply in search of each story's identity, effectiveness, balance, and thematic meaning. To sit and watch your work act on an audience of peers, and then having a discussion with them afterward, closes the loop of communication and accelerates the path toward true professionalism.

> Sidebar definitions like this will appear throughout this book when important dramatic or other useful principles emerge from the examples and comments.

Accompanying each writing assignment are samples from a class of my former students. Each piece is a rapid sketch, and my commentaries should make it crystal clear that they are not models to be emulated but rather the seeds of something awaiting development.

As the assignments progress, important dramatic principles will emerge from the examples and comments. This lets you encounter the elements of dramaturgy as they naturally occur, one by one. Sidebar definitions in a special box (see the example on this page) allow you to relate definitions to examples and to locate them in context later when you need them.

The dominant mood while doing this work is one of excited enjoyment, especially if you are part of a group or class. What can be more convivial than making vital discoveries?

COURSE GOALS

Whether you use this book with one or two friends, or in a formal class, the course work will offer ways to:

- Understand and value some of the experience that has formed you.
- Articulate a developing artistic identity for yourself.
- Create screen ideas in outline or treatment form.
- Draw on a variety of sources that are personal, cultural, or observational.
- Learn the fundamentals of dramatic criteria and use them as tools to develop ideas.
- Work with others collaboratively instead of competitively.
- Give and take constructive critique.
- Initiate the creative process in a variety of ways.

If there is a single key to developing as a writer, it is to keep writing, and to keep submitting your writing to the reactions of an audience. You will therefore need to:

- Write every week. By all means write your initial work by hand if this allows greater spontaneity.

- Use a computer or typewriter for any presentation that will be read by others. If your handwriting is anything like mine, it ties up the reader's attention in word-by-word comprehension, and this obscures the larger ideas. Use your computer's spelling checker to catch typos or other anomalies.
- Have someone literate proofread your work before it goes to the class leader or group.
- Be present at every meeting. Much discovery and learning happens unpredictably there.
- Use the self-evaluation work to define your artistic identity at the outset and to review it again at the end.

The book has six parts:

Part I: *Explanation* of the book and its goals; its approach to the creative process and overcoming writers' impediments; explanation of its emphasis in working in outline form. This is the part you are reading right now.

Part II: *Observation, improvisation, and self-examination projects* to loosen you up and help you work up a preliminary sketch of your own creative identity.

Part III: *Creative writing assignments* that put you to work writing in outline form. They draw on resources such as autobiography, family tradition, dreams, myth, legend, news media, and short stories. Early assignments are aimed at short screen projects. Successful short work is much favored at festivals and can leverage you into being funded for longer and more demanding work. In the later assignments, you work toward a full-length documentary subject and two pieces of original fiction. One is aimed at short screen fiction, and the other at the feature film. (From Part III onward, each chapter culminates in a bibliographical section called "Going Farther" for those who want to pursue more specialized knowledge.)

Part IV: *Revisiting* your body of work to see how it modifies your ideas about your creative identity. This helps you consolidate the direction of your future work.

Part V: *Expanding your work into its final form*: it includes some basics that you will need to turn your outline into a screenplay, such as screenplay form, dialogue, structural considerations, and character development. Most criteria hold good for other forms, like prose fiction or theater.

Part VI: *For class leaders*, on how best to use this book in a course or workshop, especially if you are new to teaching idea development.

Whenever you write, remember to *create freely first, then analyze and rewrite afterward*. Your growing body of critical knowledge must never inhibit your instincts and personal voice. To this end, use any and every writing method that lets you play freely as you search. Revel in the chaos this improvisation produces; afterward you can move over to the editorial mode and organize and refine what you have produced. You will learn much from the way your mind works when it is free to follow its instincts.

GETTING STARTED

It's a good idea to read ahead in this book to see where the work is leading and what kinds of criteria and issues are coming up. Most of your writing will be in scene outline, which I will describe when the time comes to use it. Each week you will do work on your own in preparation for the next class. You will need to make four kinds of collections; start making them straight away in preparation for the work to come:

Picture File: Remove pictures from magazines and newspapers that appeal to you and save them. Strong inspiration can come from a war photograph, a human interest portrait, a silly fashion ad or a fabulous landscape.

Dream Journal: This is private, kept at home; it will be used for the Dream Sequence project. Keep a notebook by your bed so you can write down your dreams as they occur. It's important when recalling a dream not to move until you have reconstructed as much as possible. Often you will start with a fragment, but as you quietly contemplate that fragment, another and another will return until you have a fairly complete record to write down. You can train yourself to wake up and record a good dream. Before you go to sleep, tell yourself that you mean to wake up after a dream. Keep up the instructions nightly until it starts happening spontaneously.

News File: Save good news stories in a folder for use in the News Story and Documentary projects. Go through old magazines and papers, because you'll find back material that no one else will think of using. You'll need some stories collected for the News Event and Documentary sessions. A fantastic source of free newspapers and magazines is a recycling center, if they will let you rummage.

Writer's Journal: Keep a small notebook with you at all times and record the thoughts, sights, or ideas that appeal to you. Making records and squirreling away all kinds of things that attract your notice are writerly habits. Time spent traveling, waiting around, eating, or even sleeping can be turned to good account. Recording the actual is your apprenticeship in observing life more closely and astutely. Your instructor will probably ask to see your Writer's Journal at set times during the course.

These journal observations will be used to play "Instant Story" in class, and they will be a bank of ideas for your writing. It will speed retrieval of particular items if you tag each with one or more of these "CLOSAT" categorizations in the margin:

C = description of *Characters* who could be used in a story.
L = interesting and visual *Location*.
O = curious or evocative *Object*.
S = loaded or revealing *Situation*.
A = unusual or revealing *Act*.
T = any *Theme* that intrigues you or that you see embodied in life.

Definitions and Examples

C (*character*) is anyone whose appearance, mannerisms, occupation, or activities suggest potential for a person in a story. You might see somebody briefly in the street and find their image persisting, or you might sit down to distill what you know about an acquaintance of many years. Their ultimate importance will depend on what resonances they acquire as you start working with them. The characters you "collect" become your repertory cast. You may make them into bit-part players or major protagonists. Some people will be unlike anyone you have ever seen before, but many will be types. A good type description will summon a smile of delighted recognition from your listeners. The examples here are brief, or *thumbnail*, descriptions. *Character examples*: ruddy-faced factory maintenance man with a little dog for a companion; rapt little black girl with tongue out as she reads; aging biker couple with similar long, gray ponytails; woman in a yellow running outfit that makes her look like a pantomime chicken.

L (*location*) is any place that suggests a setting for something to happen. Often characters and places go together, but it can be interesting to shake things up and make your runaway urban teenager hide from the law in a smelly chicken farm, or your wan bank clerk prove himself on a doomed Russian trawler. *Location examples*: harbor bridge with a single street lamp; run-down stationery store; attic room with a grubby, unmade bed; country garage with yellowing pinups next to a rack of fan belts.

O (*object*) is any that is worth recording because it is eloquent of place, time, situation, or owners. *Object examples*: pottery pig for storing cookies; battered straw hat; valentine card that plays a tune; set of partially melted plastic soldiers; woman's makeup kit left on a park bench; pair of running shoes dangling by their laces from a dead tree branch.

S (*situation*) is a conjunction of circumstances or a predicament that puts the character or characters under some special constraint or influence. *Situation examples*: being the poor guest of a wealthy family; car breaking down at night in a scary neighborhood; being X-rayed wearing nothing but a paper gown that gapes open at the back; finding that one's neighbor in a packed cinema is an indigent person with an overpowering smell; a neighbor digging what looks like a human-sized grave in his yard.

A (*act*) is any human deed or action that seems freighted with meaning or potential. *Action examples:* nearly having a driving accident, through distraction; setting up a practical joke; running fully clothed into the sea; avoiding someone; chopping firewood; improvising a bed for the night; drawing a lot of money from a cash machine; maintaining a smile while being threatened.

T (*theme*) is the central or dominating idea, often not stated anywhere directly, underlying the subject of a story and commenting upon it. The subject of a story might be a homeless teenager, but its theme the superlative importance of kindness to strangers. *Thematic examples:* breaking boundaries; revenge; love conquers all; jealousy; betrayal; brotherly love, guilt, atonement, forgiveness.

Playing Cards

For the assignment in chapter 5 you will need to produce your best observations as index cards. With these we will play an improvisational Instant Story card game. Handwritten cards won't work; make your cards in the typed, standard format below. If it's easier, staple or gum computer print to index cards. Below is an example for a character called Ronnie. Because he's a character, he's coded C. More examples appear at the end of chapter 3.

Your initials	Descriptive tag	Code letter
P.P.R.	*Ronnie, Movie-Theater Manager*	C

Seventyish man with shock-white hair combed back in a sweep to cover his bald spot. Dressed in cheap suit pants and shirtsleeves, heavy wire-rim aviator glasses protecting his sliver eyes. Swears like a sailor at the staff of the crumbling movie palace and laments the bygone days of Hollywood and black-and-white. Greets any patron over sixty-five with a smile, scowls at all others. Smokes and sucks on coffee incessantly.

2

About the Creative Process

Discovering the source of stories you are best qualified to tell, especially the autobiographical ones, where our work starts, often comes down to finding new connections between causes and effects in your own life. It means identifying what distinguishes your life from other people's and elaborating the possible consequences. This is seldom tidy or efficient, but digging for deeper levels of awareness often leads to unexpected insights. From this one can make better and more compassionate guesses at the underlying motivations of others—both real and fictional.

Let me give an example of finding such a source that is uncomfortably close to home. A while back I had to describe my life and body of film work for a degree program. Working on the capsule autobiography part, I wrote that "the twenty or so documentary films I have directed are all different, and have nothing in common with each other." No sooner had I had set this down than I realized with a premonitory sense of shock that the opposite was true. All of my documentaries explored the same theme—that of imprisonment and the will to break out of it. Though they had a wide range of subject matter and outcomes, this concern had been lurking beneath all of them, unknown to me.

As my mind raced to explain how this could possibly be, the answer arose, just as mysteriously. I must have been marked—first as the lone middle-class boy in a hostile blue-collar village, then as the child of a foreigner. In various schools, in my family, in an England at war and besieged by Germany, I had always felt like the odd man out. Later I felt it again as a conscript in the military. All that time, the sense of being a captive must have been too habitual even to register. How logical later to make a string of films about captives and breaking out!

Reviewing how former students had developed, I saw that most people *do* take a long time to gain possession of their own sources. Only slowly and imperfectly do we comprehend the driving forces in our own lives. Yet something inside us, something waiting in the wings to be recognized, knows the situation and steers us with unswerving accuracy. How exhilarating when one finds a key, makes a new connection, and puts in place another piece of the jigsaw puzzle!

Must one wait for such keys to fall into one's hand? I think that an important part of the creative process is to search actively for them. Where, after all, does the belief and drive to create something like a story come from? It exists because you carry markings from emotional experience. You feel the impact of particular personalities and situations during your development. Your path through life is highly influenced by such circumstantial marks, which may be cultural, familial, or experiential. Even if you are as ignorant of them as I was, these stigmata direct you. But once you know more about them, you can guess at where you have been going and why. Fabricating stories from the lives around us, guided by the energy generated by our own unfinished business, leads us to long-term research into the meaning of it all. Creating is making something—maybe a painting, a poem, a story, a film. For a work to be meaningful to others, it has to go farther than merely reflecting actuality. It has to imply ideas about those people and those phenomena.

Humankind has always searched for meaning, either through religion, philosophy, or art. We hunger for it. Why do "nice guys always finish last"? Do they, really? Why do some people go to war with their neighbors? Why are some people (as I found out, making a film about conscientious objectors) ready to die rather than kill someone else?

The more we look at what remains unexplained, the more we sense where we should be looking for answers, and the more we use narrative fiction, documentary, journalism, or some other form as a vehicle for proposing questions, ideas, and possible meanings. We need not be prisoners of past experiences or see our fictional characters as such. By describing and exploring those experiences, we can posit reasons, alternatives, and choices.

Those who create successful stories always seem aware of their themes and how these arise from their unfinished business. They usually know what their quests are; they either concentrate on possible variations or are unable *not* to. People who create a range of good, expressive work often work from only one or two deeply felt themes. Being marked in such particular ways doesn't make them limited, any more than a single foundation dictates what building can go up.

For the confirmed artist, compulsion or even exorcism is operating, as Ann Lamott testifies in her entertaining autobiographical study of the writing process, *Bird by Bird: Some Instruction on Writing and Life* (New York: Doubleday, 1995). Being possessed is probably latent in you, too, if writing attracts you. Acting on the challenge takes courage. Recalling the raw material of one's life and engaging with it anew can be uncomfortable or even frightening. But inner conflict and unhappiness are normal and necessary parts of the human experience, and they denote the very dissatisfaction that turns a human life into a productive quest.

I should say, however, that if your inner conflicts are so present and so debilitating that your life seems impaired, you may need to take them to a good psychotherapist. Therapy exists to reduce pain to manageable proportions and to restore one's appetite for living. Art exists to grapple with the nature and mystery of human existence, and to share the patterns and forces of *what is* with others.

The creative process is like making models and putting them before an audience for reactions. You have to go through many attempts, follow your own intentions and intuitions, and be ready to learn from your critics. Very seldom do works spring into their full being, like Mozart's music is said to have done—and we don't know what mental processes he went through before committing his work to paper. Most people can't work for long inside their heads. They put ideas down on paper, and this allows their minds to contemplate what they have produced and to travel farther.

One has to like the process itself, for the product is often long in coming and deficient when it does come. One must be ready to make a slow, strenuous evolution. Peter Baer, a painter friend in London, said that even the most untalented person could become a decent painter if they simply worked at painting for twenty years. I would go farther and say that, within limits, anybody can become anything if they stay with the learning process and keep working toward it. Any writer will tell you that to become a writer takes a lot of writing and a lot of discipline. This approach brings its own reward in any art form. Just keep doing that art, and use your own critical standards and those of people you respect.

Why then do so many people who want to write have such trouble doing so? Usually I find that they are trying to swim against the current of their own abilities. Many are suffocated early in school by being made to write to formulas or in a dry, suffocating, pseudo-scientific style. Others have trouble when they fly to extremes of self-concept. Some expect to produce something tremendous. Others feel small and impoverished, with nothing to give; feeling that they live, figuratively speaking, in a contemptible little shack, they mourn that they don't have great mansions with a hundred rooms, like . . . and one finishes the sentence with the name of the famous, talented person one feels so close to in spirit.

But try really living in that shack. Open your eyes and look around the inside. Eventually you'll find a trapdoor leading down to a larger room below. Opening off that room, in turn, are other hidden portals. Find any one and open it, and discover more rooms, more space, more twists and turns, new panoramas, more resources. Inside is your real life—a labyrinth of stored ideas, feelings, and experiences waiting to be explored.

Analogously speaking, as I said earlier, you have already done everything, seen everything, felt everything that humankind can experience. But the hatches are battened down until you find your way to open them. Strong, communicative writing comes from the struggle to describe *what is*, not what should be. Willpower cannot alter the world nor make one other than what one is. Embrace your own path and that of your characters, whether good, bad, or indifferent.

Enough exhortation. Let the writing work you actually do make its own argument. You will begin to see what fascinates you at a deep level, what draws you back time and again. By fulfilling the varied work this book demands, you can find the outline of your own center. That center is sublime. You can approach it but never hold it or pin it down.

The course work in this book takes you high and fast over a lot of terrain; it never asks you to polish or rework a piece. That comes later, when you move from the ideation stage to expand your work into something finished. Although that process lies outside the scope of this book, keep in mind that finding a final form for anything takes many drafts. This is central to the creative process.

PART II

OBSERVATION, IMPROVISATION, AND SELF-EXAMINATION ASSIGNMENTS

———————————— *3* ————————————

Introductions and Playing "Instant Story"

This session begins with the usual introductions that inaugurate any group work and then moves to improvising a story from random elements. This will be collaborative, sketchy, and very lively. We are concerned not with competing to see who is best, but with learning what can be playfully improvised in a short time.

Several purposes are at work here. One is simply to get several people who have never met before working together. Another is to show how in just ten minutes a group can unite a chance assortment of characters, things, and places into an entertaining fragment of narrative. The message here is that if a group can do this, so can any of its individuals. Sheherazade in the *Thousand and One Nights* saves her life by delighting the king with a different story every night. She does not tell him (or us) how she does it, but her ability to improvise makes her indispensable to the king's happiness. She represents the artist beguiling us with entertainment but whose stories are freighted with such a profound view of the human spirit that we need more of them.

Some actors, comedians, and performance artists can fascinate us with their quick-witted talent for improvisation. Later, thinking over what they produced, we see additional dimensions of meaning. What matters here is not their capacity for being profound, which is a heavy responsibility, but the simpler capacity to adapt, make something good of any chance situation, and have fun doing it.

> *Improvisation* is translation of our unconsciously stored experience into action. It happens best under some special pressure and when we choose to risk trusting it.

Though we call this a talent, everybody has done it. Think back to an occasion when your friends howled with laughter because you were for once effortlessly funny, or to a time when your mind suddenly solved some intractable problem all on its own. Under the right conditions, something special happens. It's like a kite suddenly taking off. This is our intuitive self, our native intelligence at work. It is the near-perfect working of our unconsciously stored experience emerging under the right kind of pressure. But it only seems to happen when we choose to risk trusting it to work. There are no advance guarantees.

The optimal conditions for improvisation seem to be these. You are confronted with a situation that you may or may not fulfill; it is risky, and you may fail. You are in a devil-may-care mood, or you are desperate; either way, you plunge into action without forethought. You know that if you stop to think, you are sunk. So you don't think, you stay in the moment and act, letting your intuitive autopilot take care of decision making. People who play or watch fast sports know how central this human quality is to such games. Players are at their best when they can both relax and take risks. The scrutiny of the spectators either intensifies this or hinders it, according to how well the player can stay focused. It is quite plain to see when players get rattled and lose their nerve. Similarly, you can sometimes see a good actor "lose focus," or a less good one who has never found it.

The favored condition rests on abandoning the proven track, the prepared method, and all that is safe and risk free. It is achieved, as the acting teacher Konstantin Stanislavsky once explained, through focusing on the moment, on the actual, and never on the self as it performs—for then the actor becomes self-conscious, self-judging, painfully aware. Such extreme exposure is seldom required of writers, yet willingness to take emotional risks, to relax and expose one's ideas and vision, requires some of the same courage and attraction to psychic danger. It is also something that you can constantly practice in daily living. As you practice, you develop trust in your ability to create in the moment. That's why you will present your work to an audience, and why you will become an articulate audience for each other person in the class.

A good audience doesn't just judge, it also supports the entertainer. As an audience member, your job is to give support to your colleagues, tangible appreciation for every risk they take. This way, people trying to create become an ensemble, and the whole becomes greater than the parts.

Conventional education does the very opposite of all this. It puts great store on preparation, memorization, and individual competition with others. Of course, everyone must learn to read and write, and master a basic body of information, but for much that matters in life, conventional education is more a hindrance than a help. It teaches us to take the safest path, the one of least resistance, and leaves us desperately unable to speak from the heart in public. The work we will be doing will go in another direction. See if you like it.

Since today all the groups work from the same materials, we'll see how differently each group imagines. Afterward you will discuss from an audience viewpoint what lay behind the improvised fragments.

CLASS ASSIGNMENT

1. *Introduce yourself* in five minutes or less, saying who you are, where you come from, and what interests, obstacles, or difficulties have led you to be interested in an idea-development class. Also say what kind of work particularly attracts you. It may be short fiction films, documentaries, television journalism, or it may be what draws most people—writing feature films.

2. *Divide into groups of three or four persons.* You may stay in these groups for the whole course or change groups later. At each session the group elects a different person to act as secretary. This person takes notes on discussions and reports the group's work back to the class.

3. *Play "Instant Story."* You have ten minutes to invent a scene from several given ingredients:
   a. Put photocopies of the twelve cards at end of this chapter in a hat; someone on behalf of the whole class blindly picks cards

   > A *scene* is an episode or a sequence of events usually taking place in one locale or in one stretch of time.

   until there is one location, one object, and two characters. Today, this set will be used by all the groups.
   b. Each group now puts their heads together for ten minutes to improvise collaboratively a scene that brings these three elements together. The group secretary takes notes.

4. *Reconvene the class.* Group secretaries describe the scenes that their groups made up. This is usually a lot of fun, and it shows how imaginative and different stories can be when developed from a common starting point.

5. *Break into groups.* Based on the scenes just recounted, take fifteen to twenty minutes to *develop criteria for good story ideas and good critical feedback.* Again, the secretary takes notes of the discussion. Each group consider:
   a. What makes a story effective for the listener?
   b. How should one describe a story idea? What language, similes, or groupings might one use to classify or communicate it?
   c. What constitutes helpful feedback for the writer?
   d. What is least helpful and to be avoided?

6. *Reconvene the class.* Consider all the answers to each question, with each group's secretary giving its answer in turn. We're interested in where groups thought differently and what ideas they held in common. Discuss, as time allows. Someone should be designated to keep notes and write up a manifesto of the ideas and principles that emerge, making a copy for each class member.

GENERAL DISCUSSION

If time permits, you might want to discuss all or any of the following:

1. In which stories did the given characters particularly come alive and why?
2. In which stories was there some kind of conflict, something for a main character to push against?
3. Which stories brought their stories to a satisfactory conclusion, or "resolution"?
4. Which stories or parts of stories were fresh and managed to avoid stereotypes?
5. Which story most left you wondering, "And what happens next?"

> *Conflict* is the struggle between forces that determines the action in drama. Conflict can be *external conflict*, existing between characters or between a character and natural law or fate. Conflict can also be *internal*, a character going through an inner struggle to arrive at a difficult decision.

> The *resolution* to a dramatic situation is whatever action concludes and resolves the situation's conflict.

Getting the class, either as individuals or as groups, to critique, solve problems, and formulate working principles is very important. Here the class does most of the discovery work. I am always impressed by the sheer wisdom that any group can produce, particularly when people have become really comfortable with each other. This is the very antithesis of the lecture method, where the thinking and the answers are delivered by the "expert" to an essentially passive class. Discussion takes longer, but each member contributes, and each uses his or her own mind to gain practice and make himself (or herself, of course) into a proficient dramatist.

CARDS FOR PLAYING INSTANT STORY

Characters

> *MGH*   *Rita, Distressed Yogi*   C
>
> Beside her constant stretching and movement, this fortyish woman wears the stress and discomfort of a week's trouble upon her brow. Her smooth, black Lycra body suit and deep purple sweater contrast with the sagging lines of her forlorn face. Her gestures are graceful but vain.

SNW *Uncle James* C

Has half an index finger. Holds his vodka bottle with pride and is rejuvenated by the first sip. Walks with a slight stagger. Most people know him. Some wave. Couldn't care less about others' perceptions of him. Has insightful conversations and is reliable for a good laugh. A tattered survivor living mostly in the streets. Needs a hug on occasion. Lonely eyes.

AJM *Kid with Dinosaur* C
Obsession

Restless boy of nine. When not thumbing through books on paleontology, he hunts in the backyard for dinosaur bones or any clues the giant lizards might have left behind. Keeps a docile iguana named Spike near him most of the time, usually on his shoulder. His parents have nearly given up hope on their son and his all-consuming passion.

BAB *Leonardo Zaccanti,* C
Mob Boss

Huge, obese fifty-six-year-old man in a white suit. Often sits in an ugly relic of a chair from the seventies, smoking a cigar. Likes to click through the TV stations looking for something good, like *Miami Vice*. Laughs at witty things he says to himself in Italian.

Objects

ACG   *A Postcard*   O

Fresh and new, with no postage and no date. On the front is a Confederate flag, and the back reads, "Keys are with Jay." There is no postmark or return address.

MGA   *Somebody's Black Glove*   O

Black leather, dulled from harsh conditions, lying lonely in the gutter. Thumb and forefinger worn so low that barely a translucent skin has survived. Charcoal ashes coat the crevices between the fingers; the smell of peanut butter emanates from the whole glove.

PPR   *Dancing Clown*   O

The small, primary-colored box rests quietly on the counter top, one side open like a diorama. Inside is a garishly smiling clown with elastic limbs frozen in a jig, his arms and legs bent unnaturally. Later the box will be wound, and he will be summoned to perform, jerking spasmodically.

KDL   *Arizona Dream Poster*   O

A big poster titled "Arizona Dream." In the center is a big fish flying up into the sky. At the right upper side we see the moon, and behind the fish is a huge cactus, standing in the vast, spreading desert.

Locations

MH   *Freight Elevator*   L

A freight elevator, the kind only used for moving large things, in an old tea factory. Two sides are not enclosed. It is a platform that rises through space . . . grey, cold. You can see great black cables all the way to the top, where they melt into darkness. Precarious-sounding groans are heard in the darkness as the grey floors go by.

JP   *Narrow Walkway*   L

A narrow walkway between a park that is next to a river on one side and, on the other, a four-lane highway filled with speeding cars. Newspapers and plastic bags are flying in the strong wind made by the cars. There are a few thin trees, which don't have any leaves. No one is in the park.

TGO   *The Uncrowded Restaurant*   L

The walls are all painted a very light pink. There is only one huge window, which shows all the cabs driving on Third Avenue. Long, thin mirrors cover the other wall. The waiters, all wearing black vests and white shirts, sit at the table nearest the kitchen. They look bored. The sound of the street is all that can be heard.

| MGA | A Shack | L |

A green meadow, then the lush foliage of trees and flowers of many colors. A crystal blue stream runs alongside the road, which has become a narrow cobblestone path. Behind ten feet of dirt, a shack composed of trashed wood panels and rusty nails stands proud. Classical music comes from within the shack.

Autobiography and Influences

PREPARATION

The aim in these preparatory chapters is to arrive at a provisional description of what your life, tastes, and passions have equipped you to write about well. Three of the assignments in later chapters require a personal response—a story from your childhood, one told in your family, and story materials that you have dreamed. There is a chicken-and-egg dilemma here: one needs a creative purpose in order to write a story, but one must write in order to uncover a creative purpose. To minimize the problem, this chapter contains some self-assessment work that will help you fashion a profile of your artistic identity.

To do this, you will review the areas of your life that may have marked you, and after that, you will look at people who have especially affected you. Some will be people you know well, others not. We acquire important parts of ourselves because of special people, who can be actual or fictional. Their function is to show us how to become more authentically ourselves.

Autobiographical Survey

From the following prompts, make brief notes of anything that has left a deep mark—for good or bad—and that seems specially significant to the person you are now:

1. *Beginnings:* year and place you were born, special circumstances and conditions, special religious or social conditions, your parents and any unusual circumstances.
2. *Health:* Special events, accidents, diseases, health circumstances.
3. *Early influences:* Special friends, visitors, neighbors, local characters.

4. *Relations:* Any siblings, cousins, grandparents, uncles, aunts who played a special role in your life.
5. *School:* Schools you attended, special courses, influential teachers, special events or traumas, special friendships or antipathies.
6. *Special activities:* Jobs, tasks at home, membership in group activities or sports.
7. *Journeys:* Any memorable migrations, travels, holidays, escapes, or quests by your family or yourself.
8. *Adolescence:* For most people this is a war zone. What was most at stake for you?
9. *Major conflicts:* What have been the major conflicts in your life?
10. *People you have loved:* These can be family members, your first love, or those you fell in love with subsequently. What did you learn?
11. *People you have hated:* People to whom you have or had a strong aversion. When was it, and why? What did you learn?
12. *Vocation:* Work you trained for or otherwise learned, or work you were made to do.
13. *Avocations:* Work that you wanted to do, such as hobbies, crafts, special interests.
14. *Arts:* Special experience or influences that turned you on to the arts—music, movies, plays, books, poetry, authors, movies, movie directors, etc.
15. *Beliefs:* Religious or philosophical ideas or believers that influenced your path.
16. *Celebrations:* Any memorable special events, festivals, or reunions.
17. *Life's lessons:* Experiences, whether troubling or uplifting, that have deeply marked you and have altered your direction.
18. *Future:* Plans, hopes, and fears that you have at the moment.

Keep your answers in mind when you do the next assignment. They may be very helpful. Unlike the autobiographical assessment, the next is for an oral presentation to the class.

Find Your Alter Egos

You can approach your deeper identifications by uncovering those characters with whom you resonate. The aim is to supplement what you did in the previous exercise. One person near the top of my list would be a nurse that I met while making a documentary about volunteers in the Spanish Civil War. Faced with a corridor of seriously wounded soldiers, she had to choose the few who would come under the care of the only surgeon. Though very young, she was suddenly faced with tragic responsibilities, and she lost her youth at a stroke. Thirty years later, she wept when speaking about it; she could never feel assured that she had made the right choices. Probably she resides in my memory because her story epitomizes experiences of my own as a young adult—walking unprepared into major choices and responsibilities, and feeling haunted ever after by the pathetic inadequacy of my responses.

1. List six or eight *characters* from literature, cinema, or theater with whom you feel a special affinity. An affinity can be hero-worship, but it becomes more interesting if your response is to darker or more complex qualities in personalities or situations. Arrange them by their importance to you.

2. Do the same thing for *public figures*, like actors, artists, politicians, sports, or historical figures.

3. List *people you know* who have had a strong and direct influence on you. List those with bad influences as well as the good—but leave out immediate family members, as they usually overcomplicate the exercise.

PRESENTATION

Speak for no more than five minutes, describing your top person in each of 1, 2, and 3 above, focusing on the qualities to which you resonate in each.

DISCUSSION

Discuss impressions either as a class or as groups reporting to the class. Here are some suggested topics:

1. What did you notice as common themes?
2. Were there themes common to the speakers' gender?
3. What stays in your memory as special and unusual?
4. Who did you find yourself admiring for their frankness, and what did this person or people say that particularly impressed you?
5. Whom did you feel you came to know best as a result of their presentation?

---5---

Observing from Life

Writers and actors work to develop acute observational skills, because the source for all their work is the extraordinary profusion of characters and events to be found in actuality. You will be practicing these skills and some methods for collecting and sorting what might be useful to your writing.

To show how such observations can lead to stories, we're going to play an improvisational story game. Its value is that:

- You get to know others in the class.
- You see how other people's minds work.
- You see how a group can produce and synthesize ideas.
- You get to see your intuition in action and learn to trust its abilities.
- You learn that the ability to sketch fast is as valuable to writers as to graphic artists.
- Each story has its own form that can be usefully discussed.
- Each story has problems that invite solving.
- Each story could be extended.

CLOSAT ASSIGNMENT

Preparatory Work: The Writer's Journal

Some preparations are necessary, because this assignment culminates in a class game. If you haven't started yet, look around you and *make notes on characters, locations, objects, situations, acts, and themes* in a pocket-sized notebook, as outlined in chapter 1, "Preparations." This is your writer's journal. Keep it with you at all times so you can record appealing thoughts, sights, or ideas before they vaporize. You will recall that it's helpful for retrieving particular items later to tag each observation with one of these "CLOSAT" categorizations in the margin:

C = descriptions of a *Character* who could be used in a story.
L = interesting and visual *Location*.
O = curious or evocative *Object*.
S = loaded or revealing *Situation*.
A = unusual or revealing *Act*.
T = any *Theme* that intrigues you or that you see embodied in life.

Refer back to chapter 1, "Preparations," for definitions and examples.

From your writer's notebook now *make six "Instant Story" playing cards,* two each for Characters, Locations, and Objects. Reduce your observations to brief, telling detail rather than scattershot inventory. Code each card at the top with your initials, its type, and a tag line, like the sample cards in chapter 3. Everyone brings their six cards to class.

Play Instant Story

- *Divide into groups.* Each group pools its cards as heaps of characters, locations, and objects. The codings and tag lines make grouping easy.
- *The instructor gives each group another group's cards,* face down. Someone from each group randomly draws two from the Character pile and one each from the Location and Object piles. The idea is to start without possibility of preconceptions or preparation.
- *Play Instant Story,* taking only ten minutes for discussion.
- *Each group secretary recounts what cards the group got and what story they developed.* The class will learn with delight what each group has managed to do with a roll of worn-out orange shag carpeting, a shy young woman gospel singer, and a postal truck driver with his leg in a cast—*and* it must all happen on a mountain footpath in the early morning mist!
- If time permits, *play another round of Instant Story,* this time with three new characters, two new objects, an act, and a theme. This story will have two scenes.

Discussion

So long as these issues get discussed, their order isn't important.

- We generally recall best what engages us. Which group's story and characters does the class remember best? You may want to concentrate on analyzing this story alone.
- Of these characters, which does the class feel it knows best, and why? (A little highly selective information

Memory effortlessly winnows out the best elements from any mass of story materials, discarding all else. Let your powers of recall be your guide.

can mean much more than a lot of bland detail.)

> Use *brief, colorful, pithy description* for your dramatic detail. Less is more.

- Which story seemed the strongest, and why?
- Which story had the most satisfying development, and what was its nature? In the kind of quickly improvised fragments you've produced today, we cannot be too critical, but it's probably plain that we are left unsatisfied when two characters meet but stay in an unchanging situation. It's real, but it isn't compelling.
- What made one character the most compelling? (It usually has something to do with that character's being active, having an agenda of some kind, and *trying to get or do something*.)

> *Active characters are always trying to do or get something,* usually something subtle and concealed, as in real life.

- How functional was the location? Novice writers often conceive human interactions taking place without regard to their settings. But the mood and meaning of a setting affect us in powerful ways, both suggesting action and limiting it in useful ways. This makes the onlooker feel more connected to the protagonist's situation and able to infer his or her emotions.

> *Intriguing settings* help to define characters and augment their predicaments.

- Decide for each story who was the "point of view" character. In most narrative forms, whether literary, theatrical, or cinematic, there is usually a main character or characters through whose experiences we perceive the events. But even when a movie profiles one major character, our attention and feelings are often routed through others. Point of view, whether single or multiple, is a difficult but important aspect of storytelling. In first drafts it is often unclear who the main character is—or should be. Find him or her by asking this simple question: "In this story, who has the most potential to learn something and grow, however minimally?"

> A *point-of-view (POV) character* is one whose experiences, feelings, or attitudes mainly shape our perception of the scene. POV can be routed through minor characters for dramatic effect or convenience. Some most interesting POV characters, such as the despised Heathcliff in *Wuthering Heights*, are made *unreliable* through subjectivity brought about by anger, youth or other perceptual handicaps.

- Did any of the characters in any of the stories develop—that is, did anyone learn something and change? Evident from the most ancient recorded tales is that audiences yearn for someone in a story to learn and change, no matter how small and symbolic that change may be. In the language of drama, it is called a character's *development*. We look for it because, seemingly, of our primal longings for reasons to hope. When stories fail it is often because the writer has depicted unchanging characters.

> A character is said to *"develop"* when he or she learns enough from their experiences to make a significant change of behavior and action in situations. When young writers seem pessimistic or myopic in this respect, it is probably because present issues in their own lives seem unyielding. But even glaciers move.

Only a small, symbolic action at the end of a difficult situation is needed to suggest that change is under way or at least possible. For instance, a story about a family in crisis might end with the young main character washing her own dishes or defiantly going out in wet weather in unapproved shoes. Such actions, though limited, may indicate that she accepts that she must not only assert herself but make some compromises. We understand that she has kept her spirit and will adapt and eventually prosper. Even though such actions take place in strife and heartbreak, they can still be richly satisfying. Rebirth, after all, usually happens in doubt and pain.

GOING FARTHER PART 1

We have only used Characters, Locations, and Objects in today's session. If you didn't already discover it, there is a rich usefulness in objects and acts; they often connote meaning far beyond what they actually are.

If time permits, spin in a Situation, Act, or Theme to enrich the

> *Denotation and connotation.* A picture of an hourglass *denotes* an old form of clock, but by suggesting the sands of time running out it *connotes* mortality. Through artfully building contexts, the author can invest prosaic objects, events, or characters with poetic meaning that transcends their everyday appearances.

brew. Instant Story is a terrific warm-up exercise for starting each session and an excellent refresher when discussion extends too long and faces glaze over with fatigue. I keep the whole class's cards on hand and spring a round of Instant Story whenever change or refreshment are needed.

A variation is to make a card selection for several people and then ask them to come up with a story straight away, with no preparation time at all. This should be kept for halfway through the course, when everyone is comfortable.

Another way to do it is to put up a set of CLOSAT cards (say three characters, two locations, three objects, and a theme) and then, after a pause, spin a pencil on the floor to see who has to tell a story. This can be done a number of times. Everyone has to grab for a story, because nobody knows who the pencil will designate.

Similarly, ask everyone to bring in two (properly coded) images for each of the CLOSAT categories. Pin the pictures up in different orders—try putting all the characters together, all the locations, all the situations. Or, try selecting people to juxtapose their images in a way that has special meaning to them. Stories can be originated by groups or by individuals, according to whatever rules the class or group adopts.

The novelist John Fowles began two of his novels from the mystery of a single image. Living by the English Channel in Lyme Regis, he saw a lone woman staring out to sea toward France. She lodged in his imagination, and slowly she became the rebel Victorian governess Sarah Woodruff, deserted after an affair with a French lieutenant and destined to become the fatal attraction to the engaged and conventional scientist Charles. The enormously popular novel that emerged was *The French Lieutenant's Woman*. Another, about Mother Lee and the Shakers, arose from a mental image of a party, one of them a woman, in eighteenth-century dress riding in the half dark across a hillside.

Images, either based on actuality or imagination, are what fill our heads. Interrogating, joining, counterpointing, or extending them leads to stories. Of course, images are the lexicon of the cinema, so make every use of found images that you can. Your CLOSAT observations and images will be a vital resource when you come to tackle original fiction assignments, and these and your news clippings will jog your mind when you do news and documentary projects.

GOING FARTHER PART 2

If you like improvising from randomly generated elements, try the games in the books below. If there are terms that you don't understand, use their indexes to locate explanations.

Biro, Yvette, and Marie-Geneviève Ripeau, *To Dress a Nude: Exercises in Imagination*, Dubuque, Iowa: Kendall Hunt, 1998. (A structured approach to developing stories from found artifacts, such as a photograph, painting, or piece of music, and an alternative approach to screenwriting in its own right.)

Rabiger, Michael. *Directing: Film Techniques and Aesthetics*, 2d ed. Boston: Focal Press, 1997, pp. 152–154. (After several tosses of a coin, you may find yourself asked to write a three-character, four-minute comedy scene called "Embarrassing Moment," set late at night, with a main character the same age and gender as yourself, the main conflict being internal to one of the other characters, and the scene's crisis to be placed near the beginning.)

Spolin, Viola. *Improvisation for the Theater*. Evanston, Ill: Northwestern University Press, 1963. (Reprinted many times. A classic and extremely influential text. Though meant for theater work with children, its methods hold for people of all ages. Its philosophy lies behind Second City, Chicago's famous school of improv comedy, which has produced actors, comedians, and directors of stellar repute.)

---6---

Artistic Identity

A central tenet of this book is that each of us is branded by particular experiences that have left us with unfinished business in life that we need to somehow complete. I think of this bundle of mysterious proclivities as one's artistic identity. It exerts a major influence, and because of it we tend to engage with particular activities, people, and predicaments. Whether we know it not, each of us is engaged in a quest that we can resist or delay, but not evade.

> *Artistic identity* is the source of creativity that each person carries within. Shaped by temperament and biographical circumstances, it sends one on a quest for answers to the "unfinished business" in one's life.

Because this book is about ideation, the work you do can become important steps along this journey. First, you will profile your creative identity. The results will be provisional and may seem rather unreal. As the sojourn lengthens and you stockpile narrative ideas, something more defined will

> *Ideation* is the process of giving birth to, and developing, the fundamental ideas underpinning one's creative activities. A good idea is like a good foundation for a building—strong, deep, and singularly appropriate for what it must support.

emerge. Once this happens, ideation should become easier, because you can follow the grain of your own deepest interests.

Recognizing better where you belong emotionally and ideologically will also set useful boundaries. You can limit yourself to exploring only those areas that hold out a prospect of discovery and growth for you, and thus make optimal use of your time and energy.

A delightful irony is emerging here. During the search for one's influences, the most negative events and hated influences often emerge as crucibles for one's most valuable and intelligent realizations. Knowing this, you can begin to regard old enemies and troublesome scars as friends in disguise. What would we know without them? Like day and night, human truth contains light and dark. The "negative" is no less valuable than the "positive," because there is no good or bad human truth. All verity is complex and inter-dependent, and it is often contradictory. Hewing to this as a writer is a fas-cinating responsibility. If it awakens old pains, remember that Discomfort was ever a good teacher.

Though I may seem to be advocating self-exposure, nothing I have actu-ally described leads necessarily toward public confession. What matters is to capture the flavor of the human condition as you know it. Your audience is always moved by well realized and deeply felt themes, and it does not necessarily care about how you acquired them. So you don't have to display the exact and embarrassing experiences that may have taught you most—though this too may have its time and place.

ASSIGNMENT

Preparation

Make some notes, because you will be making a brief classroom presenta-tion. This preparatory writing can remain private. Note down:

1. The main marks left on you by your one or two most formative experi-ences. Keep description of the experiences to the minimum; concentrate on specifying their effects.

2. Two or three *themes* that might emerge from the marks that this charac-ter carries.

3. Five or six very *different characters, or types, toward whom you feel unusual empathy*. These can be people you still know, people no longer alive or in your life, or even characters in fiction to whom you strongly resonate.

Example:
   (1) "When my father came home from the war, my mother seemed to switch her attention away from me to him. He took it for granted, and he ended up closest to my older brother. So I felt increasingly isolated and assumed that anything difficult in life was something one had to face alone."
   (2) Though isolation breeds self-sufficiency, it also brings an inability to fit in; loss can give a person the energy to fight; good works sometimes start from pain and wrong.
   (3) Other characters or types:
      • Men who have trouble with women and intimacy.
      • A friend who evades his difficulty with intimacy by putting all his energies into the environmental protest movement.
      • An older woman in a fight with her boss because he wants to replace her with a younger woman.

- People in situations of crisis because of their overcontrolled emotions.
- Loners who construct self-contained worlds.
- People who instinctively swim against the tide and distrust all authority.
- Anyone searching for something or someone they have lost.

4. Three or four *provisional story topics,* as different as possible. Choose stories that reflect the concerns to which you are already committed; make all of them explore one of your themes. To mask a story's provenance, use the device of *displacement.* Move your story away from its origins by changing the gender of your protagonists or by setting the story in new surroundings or in a different time period.

> *Displacing* your underlying concerns into other areas of life lets you avoid the quicksands of autobiography. Now you can explore fresh circumstances with eyes already knowledgeable in the underlying truths.

Examples: Someone whose existence is made difficult by having to keep their real identity secret, such as a gay person in the military; someone entering a new situation who feels unacceptably different; someone suffering an ethical crisis over the validity of their work; the kind of embattled person who always thinks he has truth and right on his side, but doesn't; someone who is forced into a lesser role and must find ways to prove their value to themselves or others.

Presentation: Storytelling Goals

You are going to present your writing goals orally to the class. Before you do that, here are a couple of issues that you will probably encounter as you prepare:

- Since you probably cannot avoid being the hero or antihero (or heroine, of course) of your own life, what would make your story balanced or unbalanced, largely or only partially true, even when it is displaced away from autobiography?
- What should you tell but probably won't? Why, truthfully, should you keep silent about one point and not another?

> One's *themes and artistic identity* are the inner forces compelling one to search throughout life for answers to one's unfinished business. The storyteller develops this quest by making tales that investigate its essentials. This is for him- or herself, and also for all those who care about the same human issues.

Internal debates like this make writing a dynamic occupation, one in which everything that matters remains in flux. Remember, only you can judge what is right for your presentation.

Four-Minute Oral Presentation

Make your presentation by completing each of the sentences below. Speak from notes, rehearsing and timing your presentation beforehand.

- Two *peculiarities* of my life that have made me see with special eyes are. . . .
- Two *major conflicts* I have experienced in my life are. . . .
- Two *themes* that I'd like to work with are. . . .
- Two *types of person with whom I always empathize* are. . . .
- Two *story topics* to which I am presently attracted are. . . .
- Two *changes I'd like to make in my audience's consciousness* are. . . .
- Two *other important goals* I have in mind as a storyteller are. . . .

In your talk, avoid hazarding who you "are" and instead concentrate on *what you are looking for and how you intend to act on the world.* As a writer, you elect to play a part, a role that you are always developing and extending. When something seems incomplete or illogical in that role, feel free to extend or modify it imaginatively. You are developing a provocative part to play in your future work, not making an iron commitment to objective truth. Playfulness has an important place in making art.

MORE ON THE ARTISTIC PROCESS

As we have said, the storyteller agenda you have just outlined will eventually bring you closer to an inner self that is searching for its way. It works like this. Your particular life has given you a special understanding of certain forces and the way they work. Setting out to show them in action and giving shape to what you feel about them gradually releases further understandings. This inner dialogue about cause and effect, and the realizations it shakes out, is what feeds the creative process and drives it forward. It is cyclical and endlessly fascinating; it reveals itself to all who are interested.

The ultimate aim for the artist is not to self-administer therapy or generate autobiography (though these may happen) but to use one's own experience as a vehicle for grasping more of the human story and more of the inner lives of others.

Nonfiction works are also stories. In the kind of documentary work I have done, there is a clear cycle at work. It begins with the same kind of research that fiction writers often do. Gaining entry to a particular world inhabited by particular people in actual situations is sometimes lengthy and demanding. As trust grows and as people begin letting you see their lives, you get clues. These lead to discoveries, discoveries lead to breakthroughs, and breakthroughs are what ultimately reward you with larger ideas and insights. This process continues during the filming and in the editing until you sense that you have developed your story materials as much as your insight and interest permit. With each film you hope to gain further insight and ideas about your special interests, as well as a new sense of direction for the next work you would like to do. I have never been disappointed yet.

Every piece of artwork has important similarities, whether it's writing, painting, a short story, documentary, or fiction film. It is both a means of exploration and a key opening gates on the onward path.

Telling our stories to creative partners is a prelude to telling them to an audience. To find and act on the self-discovery material in this chapter might mean taking a chance or two—showing something special about yourself, trusting that the experience will lead somewhere. Having the class listen to your intentions and react as an audience is vital to discovering and accepting what you really want to do. Anyone wanting to excel in the arts cannot remain safely hidden. In your circle you will see some who are afraid to show themselves and others ready to go out on a limb. A good-hearted class supports and appreciates those who take these risks. Gradually even the shyest come forward, and sometimes they get the most support.

If you are to become involved in writing, you will need a strong notion of your own preferences for another reason as well. Film is a collaborative world, and there are social pressures that you must sometimes resist. In fiction filmmaking, the script is the film's architectural plan; like any artistic agenda, it emerges from a creative identity at work among other creative identities. In filmmaking, as in theater or journalism, one must strongly define one's own point of view, or see one's prerogatives plucked away by stronger-willed colleagues, actors, or crew members. A writer or director must work to find a clear sense of direction, if he or she is not to lose belief in their work's meanings.

> *Collaborating* with other people is a wonderfully social and energizing way to make something. Plays were once produced as a collaborative effort, and for hundreds of years there were no directors in the theatre. The preeminence of the cinema in the twentieth century may be because work of a high order has always come from group collaborations. Collaboration can, however, be a danger, if the individual gets advice from many people and cannot retain a clear sense of his or her purpose.

DISCUSSION

In today's class session, listen and react as nonjudgmentally as possible. It is still early in the process, and many are still in a fragile position. Even when you detect elements of self-defense or self-promotion, try to absorb and memorize all that people say about themselves. Limit discussion to spotting trends in how people spoke, or to grouping the stories. This is a time to build the ensemble, not tear it down. Concentrate on being constructive.

GOING FARTHER

Works on the artistic process as it affects the writer are:

Cameron, Julia. *The Artist's Way: A Spiritual Path to Higher Creativity.* New York: Putnam, 1992. (Highly prescriptive and particularly addressed to those suffering "blocks, limiting beliefs, fear, self-sabotage, jealousy, guilt, addictions, and other inhibiting forces.")

Lamott, Ann. *Bird by Bird: Some Instructions on Writing and Life.* New York: Doubleday, 1995. (Funny and engagingly personal description of the stages a writer goes through, and of the neuroses from which many writers suffer.)

PART III

CREATIVE WRITING ASSIGNMENTS

A Tale from Childhood

From here on, you start writing. The goal in this chapter is to produce something simple and direct from your memory of childhood. There are no other requirements, except that you present an event that made a strong impact on you and that you remember very clearly. From this we will examine how memory works and whether it has uses beyond simple playback. Childhood tales have the self at their center and are invariably in the first person, while most narratives are in the third person.

In this chapter, as in many others, I have included undergraduate writing examples from an idea development class that I taught at New York University. View each of these writings purely as someone else's response to the assignments. They are emphatically *not* meant to be models. Any such emulation would utterly defeat our central purpose, which is to get you writing your stories in your own way. They are examples that allow me to make an analytical commentary so you can see dramatic analysis and its tools at work, and begin using them yourself.

The NYU examples are published by kind courtesy of the writers; any unauthorized use of them whatever would be a serious infringement of their rights.

ASSIGNMENT

Describe an Event from Childhood

Briefly write up an event from your childhood that is powerful in memory. If possible, choose one you haven't told before and whose meaning is still ambiguous. The purpose is to venture into new territory, rather than retell what is safely familiar. Try to stay true to what you can see with your inner eye, neither imposing on its pictures nor resisting any form it wants you to adopt in the telling. Include your feelings if you remember having them, but don't be surprised if powerful memories seem composed entirely of images, events, and actions, with no "me" at their center.

Now Analyze the Story

What meaning will an audience ascribe to the story as you have set it down?

Creative writing is both a left-brain and right-brain activity. It requires daring, intuition, and speedy responses as one grabs for the diamonds in the rough. However

> The *inner eye* is the (often silent) cinema in your head. It replays the material of memory in a starkly truthful way. Though the inner eye may not be a factually accurate record of the original events, this is immaterial, because it represents, faithfully and powerfully, the way you now perceive them. If you work at developing the courage and skill to write what your inner eye shows—without mediating or cushioning its visions—you will write strongly. The inner eye sets the same standard of emotional truth even when you write fiction.

messily you set things down, once they exist on paper you can turn to finding order and making intellectual sense. Most people who find writing difficult are paying too much attention to the latter activity at the expense of the former, on the packaging rather than the contents of the parcel. The writing in this course is concerned with bold sketchwork, not with attaining an industrially polished end product.

Don't be distressed if you and your classmates produce work that is less refined than you see below. In the interests of making their texts easy to read, I have silently edited the typos, spelling mistakes, and syntactical hindrances that are inevitable in fast, early-draft work. As their teacher, I also come off rather better than I perhaps deserve: my accompanying notes are fuller than I could possibly give the writers at the time. I have benefited from hindsight, from being able to give each piece an unusual amount of attention, and from the class discussions that followed; all of that leads to a richer and more diverse commentary than any individual can produce.

If my comments seem overly critical or short on praise or encouragement, it is because each piece is necessarily in its infancy. Development work should get encouragement in class, of course, but your commentary should focus on potential, options, and development. Never forget that anyone can become a good storyteller—literally, anyone who is ready to work at it.

EXAMPLES

Many childhood memories preserve those awful moments when one unwittingly crossed adult demarcation lines or broke taboos whose existence one had never guessed.

Example 1 (Vilka Tzouras)

A young girl with short hair and skinny legs runs down the school hallway muttering words in a foreign language. She's running around trying to organize for a young boy to show his pipi to the girls. Although no one seems to know what she is saying, they all seem to understand. Finally she manages to round up five to six girls and without much effort convinces the boy to pull down his pants and show his goods.

They're all standing in a semicircle around him. Oohs and aahs as they all inspect the sights. The boy suddenly feels flustered, puts his penis back in, and runs into the hallway, where he starts running around in circles. A minute later he is on the floor screaming. He's just broken his leg. They all run up and look at him without saying a word. Finally, he's taken away by the school nurse, and the girls return to the classroom.

For all its apparent objectivity, this brief account has disturbing overtones. Nobody can understand her, but the skinny foreign girl with the boyish haircut manages to set up an engrossing event for her girlfriends. It concludes with the innocent victim of their natural curiosity going into a self-destructive paroxysm. By their actions the girls, silent and guilty as murderers, seem to realize that they have broken a major taboo. Like a deadly sin, it brings swift and fateful punishment.

The event is surreal, because it unfolds like a conspiracy—without language or even much sound until the boy breaks out screaming in pain. The piece is highly visual; it withholds all mention of feelings, which somehow heightens its tension and horror.

The author writes,

> From my point of view the story is extremely enigmatic but I will attempt to suggest some possible underlying themes: A young woman discovers her gender; curiosity, and what happens when you are too curious for your own good; sexuality—what can be said and what can't (taboos).

Painful early memories often include feelings of guilt and extreme isolation. Generally their turning points are the mysteriously vicious moments at which the child realizes what is forbidden, what one must *not* do.

Example 2 (Alex Meillier)

Nine years old. I avoided my weekly baths like the plague. Perhaps I had a near death experience in the infant swimming program buried somewhere in my subconscious, but I dreaded the bath. My parents would send me upstairs to bathe and when I was finished my mother would smell me to see if I was clean. Sometimes I would splash water on my hair and come downstairs to try to fool her, but she would smell me and send me back upstairs to finish my bath.

One day I decided to impress my parents. I went into the cupboard under the sink to smell the bottles to find the prettiest smelling product. I found a bottle of Pine Sol, and poured all of it into my bath. I climbed in and washed myself thoroughly. I came downstairs and my mother smelled me. She looked at me perplexed, smelled me again, then yelled across the house for my father.

"Steven, come over here!"

My father rushed over, I was confused, I don't remember what my mother told him, but he grabbed me under my arms, swinging me off the ground and rushed me back upstairs. I was crying and screaming because I couldn't understand what was going wrong. He brought me up to the bathroom, undressed me hurriedly, ran the shower, and got undressed himself. He grabbed a scouring brush from under the sink and brought me into the shower with him.

He started to scrub my flesh pink and I screamed and screamed. After a while I stopped screaming because the scrubbing was pleasurable. I remember his penis, big and hairy, right in front of my face, jiggling with the aggressive scrubbing motion. I compared mine to my father's, then I took a pee in the shower and he scolded me, but I just laughed, and then he laughed too. When the shower was over he took out a big towel and dried me off thoroughly.

That night I had a bad dream and I yelled for my dad instead of my mom. He came into my room. I told him I was scared because the *hemen gemens* that lived in the carpet was climbing into my bed and biting me. He got out a sleeping bag and laid it in the hall right outside of my parents' room. He closed the door to his room and I slept outside of my parents' door feeling safe and loved.

In this story a child who is trying to do something good touches off frenzied alarm in his parents and becomes terrified himself. Abandoned by his mother to his angry-seeming father, the boy discovers that his "punishment" is actually his father's frantic will to save him. In dramatic parlance, this is a *plot point*, because the story is suddenly turned from one apparent direction of travel to quite another, from transgression and punishment to feverish lifesaving.

Simultaneously the boy becomes aware of his father's sexual likeness to himself, and of the difference of scale between them. His father overlooks a taboo (urinating in the shower), and the cleansing concludes with the father lovingly enfolding his son in a towel. That night, when visited by fears he appeals to his father, and because the father again responds tenderly, the boy can rest in the knowledge that he is safe and cherished.

> A *plot point* is a moment where the story unexpectedly veers off in another direction. Plot points are powerful because they divert a story that appears predictable. The art of storytelling is always to maintain tension about what will happen next.

The story evokes a fundamental doubt in childhood—do my parents love me? Not until you are in danger do you find out. When Alex sees that his father responds so ardently, he knows that this all-important figure does indeed love him. He learns this from what his father does, not through what anybody says. In life, action speaks louder than words, which is something the dramatist must remember at every impulse to write dialogue.

Example 3 (Chris Darner)

The morning was damp. It was still dark outside. The house was quiet. A shuffling coming from his parents' room. Clothes. Probably his clothes.

He stumbled out of bed, grabbed a towel and fell into the shower. The water woke him up a little but he wanted nothing more than to be back in bed, asleep, with today not being what it was, when it was. A rapping on the bathroom door interrupted his shower. He flicked off the shower head halfway to listen for words, the water still hissing in the pipes.

"You almost ready?" His mother's voice, uncomfortable.

"Yeah." He didn't feel like using any more words than he had to.

In the family room sat a black duffel bag that his aunt, an airline attendant, gave him for Christmas. Black with a single white stripe, it sat on the couch, filled with clothes. Clothes folded so perfectly that they made the bag square. Only 14 years old, he hadn't learned how to fold clothes quite that well, much less pack them so perfectly into a bag. He thought about how much he loved his mother.

"You ready?"

"Let me put on my socks and shoes." He wasn't even looking up at her. He was too afraid. Instead, he dropped down onto the couch, next to his black bag, and began to put on his socks and shoes. His socks slipped up his moist feet and ankles. His shoes felt tight when he pulled down on the laces.

He held his stare at the floor while his mother fixed coffee in the kitchen. He glanced out into the backyard and could tell by the colors of the gray brick wall that it was overcast. Dark gray sky. He locked his eyes back down on the floor in front if him. He was cold. His body didn't want to be awake.

He held his stare at the floor. He thought how it must look to his mother. How it must look as though he hated her. He wished he could tell her how much he loved her and how afraid he was. He was so afraid. He was worried to even think about how afraid he was, so he just stared down at the floor, his arms around his stomach to stay warm.

"You hungry? The doctors said you could have some juice if you want, just no food."

"No. I'm fine."

"Well. I'll go warm up the car."

"Okay. I'll just be in here."

His mother walked out to the car with her coffee, leaving the front door open behind her. He felt a coolness and looked out at the granite clouds frozen in the sky. A few minutes later his mother returned and told him the car was ready.

"You got everything?" He looked up at her for the first time since waking up.

"Yeah. All my clothes in here?"

"Yes. I packed your shirts and some shorts but I didn't know what exactly you'd need. I think you'll be wearing a gown most of the time, but we'll see. You ready?"

"Yeah." He stood and grabbed his bag and the backpack he laid out the night before.

He didn't want to linger in his house; didn't want to take a last look at anything, he just wanted to go.

The car ride up was quiet. They took their third car. A big old rust-colored Chevy Malibu Station Wagon. 1973. He remembered the model year because it was the same year he was born. The car radio didn't work, hadn't for years. The hum of the engine and the whistling of the heater would have to do.

Half way to the hospital he pulled a pair of drumsticks from his backpack. He didn't play, but he told himself they were cheap and would be fun to mess around with. Actually, he didn't really care whether he could play. If anyone saw them and asked, he could tell them "I don't really play, just goof around" but [he would] say it so that it sounded as if he played but was just modest about it.

He started to tap the drum sticks against the vinyl dashboard. The vinyl was brick red and rock hard from fourteen years of sun. The tapping increased. He was tapping quicker and quicker and eventually he couldn't get it rolling any faster. So he started tapping harder. He kept tapping, harder and harder. The drum beat quickly fell out of its rhythm and the head of the drumstick in his right hand dug into the dash with a loud crack. He put the drum sticks down into his lap and stared down at the peanut-sized hole in the dash. The car was old and had its share of scratches and dings, but there was something about that little hole he just made. He was ashamed. Ashamed and scared. His mother didn't say a word. She knew.

For the rest of the ride he just sat, staring out at all the different buildings and cars they passed. Buildings and cars filled with people for whom today was just another day.

They entered the hospital lot and pulled into an empty parking spot. Both he and his mother stepped out of the car without saying a word. One of the drumsticks was lying on the floor and the other rolled back under his seat.

"You want your drumsticks?"

"No." He paused, searching for something else to say to her. "Thanks."

This acutely observed story concerns the lonely dread one feels prior to a major trial of courage. Told in the third person, it relates how the boy discovers his mother's empathy when she lets his unintentional damage to the family car pass without comment. Like both previous stories, transgression brings knowledge—in this case that his mother knows why he went too far, and sympathizes. This proof of her love allows him to face his ordeal without the false ego-boost of the drumsticks. When you are loved by the most important person in your life, you don't have to drum up the approval of your peers.

Example 4 (Amanda McCormick)

A poor, hungry horse is standing in the backyard in the rain. The mother standing at the window with a ten-month-old baby on her hip considers the horse, and sighs. The horse has to be fed. She reluctantly goes outside and finds something for it to eat.

Finally, her daughter gets out of bed, already surly about something. The mother begins to scold her about her horse, reminding her that she has been forgetting to feed it at all for the last few weeks. The daughter explodes at her, reminding her that her authority, since she is the *stepmother*, is not that of a real mother. Then wait till your father gets home, the mother threatens. The mother tries to draw a line about the care and feeding of the supposedly beloved horse, but is met with even more anger. The daughter storms out to meet some friends at a shopping mall.

Despite the baby's wails, the house is very quiet. The mother looks out at the scraggly horse standing in the rain. She is still angry at her stepdaughter and is not going to wait on this problem a day longer. She bundles up the baby and puts her in a stroller, puts on her own coat, goes outside and leads the horse out of its pen.

The mother, the horse, and the baby start off down the road together. They pass rows of houses and rows of orange groves. Perplexed motorists honk at the sight for lack of a better reaction, but one man does stop and ask her if she needs some help. She stops briefly and shakes her head, no, and continues on her way in the rain.

When she reaches the stables she is even more determined on her course of action. She offers the horse to them free of charge and they readily agree. The mother and the baby turn back in the rain and begin the trip home.

The writer adds:

> I am the baby in this story so strictly speaking I am too young to remember it. I remember my mother telling it to me over and over when I was young, so I have come to strongly identify with it. I have a strong image of my mother, myself, and the horse on the road, probably partially invented, but nonetheless an image that has shown up in my writing. Another thing that is important to me thematically about this story is the way that so much conflict can be invested in the image of something essentially innocent, like the horse.

Although submitted as a childhood story, this highly understated piece really belongs in the next chapter, with family stories. I include it here as a testimony to the fact that under special circumstances, one's memory can appropriate something it cannot really have witnessed. Whether it would be rejected in a court of law is unimportant here, because we are looking for good stories.

This story, written in the third person and present tense, lays out the inexorable conflicts of step-family life using image and action. The stepdaughter, probably acting up because she has been displaced by a girl baby, will-fully neglects her horse. At the focus of her anger is her stepmother, who must now draw a line between what is and what isn't acceptable. Ostensi-bly she does this on behalf of the poor horse, condemned to stand hungry, wet, and neglected. But really she must assert what is right for her own future survival. Because of this, the two innocents, horse and baby, must go on a long, wet journey through an uncomprehending world.

The final act, in which the unvalued and unloved animal is given away to people who will care for it, has an implacable justice. Though the repercus-sions lie outside the story's frame, they are all too imaginable, and in this way the story continues beyond its own end.

Two stunning images stand like beacons in this piece. One is the mother's view through the window of the "scraggly" horse standing hungry in the rain. The other is the little cavalcade advancing through wet traffic—horse, baby, and the mute, implacably angry mother.

This is a revenge tragedy in miniature. As in some Greek play, the new queen must force the antagonistic princess to face up to a new authority structure, with an act that brings unpalatable consequences. Although the mother's act is justified, everyone is fated to lose. The stepdaughter loses her horse, the horse loses its home, the absent father loses his household to strife; to earn her stepdaughter's respect, the mother must at least temporarily forfeit any of her affection. In spite of all this, the stepmother plants a for-midable flag for justice. She will neither be used nor ignored in future. No wonder this story is so important in the family.

Summary

Collectively, these stories convey how a child's emerging knowledge of the world arrives in explosive bursts of discovery. Like the detonations in an internal combustion engine, these occur at times of maximum pressure. In drama as in life, the *crisis*, or *turning point*, of any situa-tion often follows a major act by a central character, as when the mother won't tolerate the horse's

> The *crisis, climax, or turning point* of a scene (or of a whole story) is the point where the main character's fortunes resolve into something appreciably better or worse. The phase that follows the crisis is called the *resolution*.

victimization any more and gives it away. From this point everything must *resolve* into a new and changed situation.

It is fascinating to see how memory preserves only experience that has future significance, and how experiential and visual the preservation often is. Three of the tales deal with facing the unexpected or the unknown, and thus with gaining new knowledge. Number 2 and 3 are about the solace of love, while number 1 is a cautionary memory underlining the retribution that follows indulging forbidden curiosity. Number 4 is particularly interesting, because it involves an appropriated memory. It concerns a deadly struggle for authority between women of different generations having rival but unstated claims on the absent father.

Childhood stories demonstrate how purposefully the memory stores its owner's or its family's main experiences, and how often these memories are archetypal and are made of images and action rather than verbal exchange. Experiential memory, like dream, almost invariably projects its major meanings through action.

DISCUSSION

- What images do you particularly remember?
- Were there any common denominators in your class's stories?
- How did the storytellers handle the first-person narrative form in their stories?
- What part did action play in the stories, and what part dialogue?
- Which were the most unusual in your crop of stories, and why?

GOING FARTHER

You might enjoy some novels that handle the subjective consciousness of young people in a masterly way:

Atwood, Margaret. *Cat's Eye*. New York: Doubleday, 1989. (This is extraordinarily acute on how it feels being a child. Particularly good on the treachery in friendships between girls.)

Dickens, Charles. *Great Expectations*, 1861. (Many paperback editions. This great novel and its extraordinary psychological insights emerged from Dickens's four-year period of unsuccessful courtship. A story of a lower-class youth in love with a banker's daughter, his novel probes the bitterness of failed love when parents manipulate their children's feelings. His lifelong sympathy for the young appears rooted in the crushing loneliness and shame he experienced as an eleven-year-old, forced to work underground in a boot-blacking factory. Meanwhile, the rest of his family went to debtor's prison, an experience magnificently displaced and transformed in *Little Dorrit*.)

Salinger, J. D. *The Catcher in the Rye*. Boston: Little, Brown and Company, 1991. (The moving American classic covers two days in the life of sixteen-year-old Holden Caulfield after he has been expelled from school and goes to New York.)

Wolff, Tobias. *This Boy's Life: A Memoir*. New York: Harperennial Library, 1990. (Superbly written memories of life with an abusive, con-man stepfather, in which the pupil catches up with the master.)

8

Family Story

Here you draw upon a story passed down in your family and begin writing in present-tense, third-person, scene-outline form.

All families tell tales that portray particular members in special situations. Usually the tales date back one or two generations; they have become oral history, because they epitomize something important in the family. Such tales evoke a family member's distinguishing characteristics, a turning point, a destiny, or other memorable circumstance. Some tales are funny and paint a trenchant portrait, others embody qualities that would be difficult to describe except in a parable. Yet others have a dark or sardonic quality that might point at inherited weaknesses, misplaced ambitions, or obstinacy in the face of great odds.

My mother used to tell such a story about my father. During the down-and-out 1930s in London, when they were newlyweds and very poor, my mother was once ill in bed and sent my father out with the last of their money to buy some food in the street market. He was gone a long time. When he returned he was holding not provisions but an ornamental silver fish-server, and he was visibly proud that he had bargained it down to an exceptional price.

Here the story triumphantly stopped. To my sister and me as young children, I suppose, it signified that, in the antediluvian times before we came along, our father had been charmingly unworldly and easily distracted. From an adult perspective, it has accrued more somber meanings. I think she was saying that he neglected her when she was vulnerable but that he had to be forgiven even when his attention wandered dangerously off the point. She also told stories about his fatherlessness and about his mother's neglect of him and abuse of his emotions when he was a hungry Paris street urchin. If my memory serves me right, those more sympathetic stories ceased before I was out of my teens.

Someone else could have told other, equally true stories about him. They might have illustrated his practicality, his blinkered tenacity in getting what he wanted, his ability to improvise much out of little, or his insatiable need to be liked by pretty women. But for reasons that illuminate my mother's choice of truths, she epitomized him as naive and boyish.

Whoever tells good stories controls historical truth. Telling a story is a way for a family member to entertain while summarizing the essentials in a few deadly strokes. It's also a way we frame each other. Frames limit the subject's freedom and hint at what lies outside their limits. Family stories can also idealize, setting an outsized expectation for following generations to compare with their own puny efforts.

How often stories were told, when, and how they changed over the lifetime of one person's telling may also tell you about family members' hidden agendas and motivations.

ASSIGNMENT

Write Up a Story Told in Your Family

Take an account handed down in your family that does not concern yourself and that might make a pithy short story. Choose one that would translate well to the screen. It can be set anywhere and at any time. Describe the incidents and establish the characters using scene-outline form (see sidebar description). Writing in brief outline, rather than in detail and at length, enables you to get the essence down on paper fast. Then you can present it for examination, much as the architect of a large building might first show a model.

Analyze Your Work

Write brief analytic notes on:

1. The story's underlying meaning
2. Any special narrative or film production problems of which you are aware.

When writing in *scene outline* form:

- Write only in the present tense, third person.
- Write in abbreviated short-story fashion and use brief, pithy descriptions.
- Describe only what will be seen and heard by the audience.
- Exclude dialogue, shot descriptions, and author's comments. Where a dialogue exchange is unavoidable, briefly summarize its contents.
- Use a new paragraph for each new scene.

It takes vigilance to stay in the present tense, third person, because we learn early to associate stories with the past ("Once upon a time. . . ."). When you finish a draft, let it sit for a day or two before rereading it. Write further drafts before you show your work to anyone, just as you would with any important piece of writing.

EXAMPLES

Example 1 (Margaret Harris)

P——, a woman in her fifties, goes with her husband on a trip to Russia in the 1960s. Her husband is a doctor knighted by the queen of England for his advancements in surgical procedures. He is a rather uptight, strict person with a constant need to criticize and control his wife. She on the other hand is an artistic and extremely talkative person who gets strange notions in her head and can't let go of them. . . .

They arrive at the hotel, and because of their wealth, their accommodations are extremely luxuriant. Their room is equipped with a beautiful crystal chandelier that hangs from the ceiling radiating a shimmering rainbow of colors. The satin walls are papered ornately, and the oak floor is covered with an exquisite Persian carpet. P—— is concerned that their room is bugged. Her eyebrows twitch nervously beneath the glow of the chandelier. It makes sense to her because her husband works for the British Foreign Office and the prominence of his position accustoms her to such impositions when they travel abroad. She begins looking around the room. She looks everywhere, and her frantic and capricious manner is unstoppable. No article of furniture is left unturned. Her long groping fingers probe every nook and cranny of the room.

This is disturbing to her husband and he becomes so upset that he decides to dine without her, as she will *not* leave the room until she has found the bug.

Her search continues to escalate more frantically, as greasy-haired and raincoated KGB officers seem to recite dogma in her ears. Having checked every possibility she finally decides that it is perhaps planted underneath the carpet. To pull the carpet up she has to remove large pieces of furniture. She does this herself, as she is by no means a small woman, six feet tall and weighing a healthy 175 pounds. Panting and exhausted, she discovers a small golden knob in the center of the room. *This* must be it, she thinks! It becomes clear that one can unscrew it. She musters all her strength to unscrew the golden plate that is on the floor.

With a sigh of relief she looks around to see that the KGB men have disappeared. However, a large crash comes from below, as well as screams. This concerns her greatly. She quickly tries to put the room back together and look as if nothing happened. Seconds later the management enters and tells her in broken English that she has unscrewed the chandelier in the room below.

Author's notes on the story's underlying meaning and importance:

- My relative P—— was always doing foolish things. This wasn't the only time something went crashing from one floor to another. Once she left the bathtub running and it fell through to the floor below.
- Paranoia can lead you to act without thinking.
- Her imagination made for great moments in life that at the time must have seemed embarrassing.
- Her marriage was so unhappy and controlled that she got out of control in other ways. . . .
- Women didn't have careers then, and so were more apt to make up grand schemes.
- This was the only way she could get her husband's attention. Even bad attention was better than none.
- She married someone like her father, also cold and aloof. This was her way of being defiant.

About themes, the author says,

- An artistic personality when crushed will find other ways to create—even scenarios that are not real.
- A truly happy person learns to trust, whereas a person who doesn't trust is more apt to be under someone's control.
- If you expect someone to act foolishly, they will.

The author's notes on how much this apparently simple story implies go very far and need nothing extra from me. I am touched by the loneliness and sadness of the unloved central character, P——, and by the way that her anxiety generates the myopic foolishness that can only increase her isolation. These are the familiar, bittersweet, comedic characters living "lives of quiet desperation." The story successfully blends farce and tragedy, an exceptional combination that comes with a rare kind of compassionate vision.

Example 2 (Amanda McCormick)

For weeks she has waited to catch a glimpse of him leaving school, shopping at the corner market, or walking home through the center of town. Then the note is passed during the final period of English Composition. Dan B——, the catch of Barstow, wants to go out with her this Friday night.

Trying to convince her strict parents that this would be a good idea is another matter. They insist on meeting this young man before he takes their daughter out.

The big night arrives. She has spent hours primping—and praying that her parents wouldn't ruin this moment by scaring away her new boyfriend. The doorbell—she races to get it. Just as she opens it, the voice of her mother comes up from the basement: "Come down here."

They inch their way down the basement steps and walk into her mother's workshop—for the mother is an avid taxidermist. To the girl's horror she realizes that at this moment her mother is *skinning a mink*.

The boy stammers while the girl registers a look of great embarrassment. Before she can figure out a way to drag the boy out of the door, her mother has charmingly engaged him in conversation. She scrapes and cuts at the skin of the mink as she asks the boy how the baseball team is doing.

The girl stands next to what might be the most attractive boy in the entire junior class, realizing that she may never be asked out again in her entire high school career.

Author's notes on the story's underlying meaning and importance:

- This is my mother's story. She always would tell it for great comedic effect, but that concealed what was probably a very painful and embarrassing memory. In a funny way, it tells the story of her parents who constantly threw up obstacles to her freedom and happiness when she was young. It also expresses how most teenagers view their parents as strange and potentially embarrassing creatures.
- If this were a movie, it would be important to convey the backstory that sets it up: what the family was like and whether this incident was a recurring type of event. It might also be difficult to convey what is going through the head of the girl as this scene is happening.
- The pathos and eccentricity of this story are what make it stick in my mind. It is often said that humor and tragedy are closely related, opposite sides of the same ever-turning coin. I find I am attracted to that very powerful comparison.

There is a gruesomely funny central image in this story—the dead animal having its beautiful skin torn off. With breathtaking economy it conveys the heroine's predicament as she feels she is being stripped and humiliated by her mother. All this takes place under the horror-stricken gaze of her beau. Because of its comments on the scene's meaning, the skinned mink is a *motif* (see sidebar definition). This is a valuable signaling device in literature, film, and other drama—in fact, wherever a surfeit of detail could distract us from noticing the central concerns.

Film, with its shifting eyelines and closeup framings, is very good at implying a character's subjective point of view. As this outline is written, we see the mink only from the girl's point of view, but we could easily be made to see it from the boy's, too. Imagine that we see his eyes dilate as he takes in what the mother is doing; now he looks up at the mother's face, looks across to his date, then back at the hands cutting and scraping at the bloody mink while their owner makes charmingly artificial conversation. Unmistakably he sees himself becoming the next taxidermy specimen, should he linger in the shadow of this weirdo family. The next object of his consciousness might well become the door.

> A *motif* is a representation—visual, aural, verbal, or musical—of something important about a character, situation, subtext, or scene. A *leitmotif* is a motif used repeatedly and associated with a dominant theme. Thomas Hardy uses red and white throughout *Tess of the d'Urbervilles* to signify the relentless violence perpetrated on his pure-spirited heroine by the men in her life who profess to love her.

Scenes are always richer when we experience multiple points of view. The two teenagers see the mother, but the mother's awareness of them is part of the tension for the viewer. We understand that the heroine, whom we see interpreting both of their actions, is losing not only "the catch of Barstow" but maybe the possibility of all future dating. This would be stronger if the power of school gossip has been *established* during the film's exposition.

> *Multiple points of view* privilege the audience with insight into the consciousness of characters other than that of the main or POV character. This evokes the multiple strands of consciousness that exist in any populated scene, and it projects a more richly imaginative experience for the audience.

For us to infer this, the piece must establish the school's pecking order and show in its early expository scenes how a student rises or falls socially (see sidebar definition of exposition).

In Amanda's mother's day, respectable girls had to wait stoically for Mr. Right to come along. A motif to express this, and one conveniently organic to the basement setting, is the spider awaiting the fly. Motifs like this arise from searching

> *Exposition*, or *setup*, is the principle of establishing the necessary framework of facts that the audience needs. These might be: day or night, time period, place, relationships, class of the protagonists, and so on. Good exposition doesn't hold up the action or draw attention to itself. It should be subtly embedded in the action so the audience doesn't notice that it is being informed.

for similes for the heroine's predicament. Did you also notice how "the catch of Barstow" has taxidermic connotations of hunting and killing? When such hints begin emerging in your work, it is not a coincidence. It means that the story knows where you should take it.

Amanda's terse, Hitchcockian tale uses a range of symbolic, allusive, and juxtapositional techniques that point toward the myth of the princess in the tower:

- The heroine stalks Dan at the beginning. When a princess went out with the hunt she was likely to see, or be seen by, the choice of her heart, the poor but handsome commoner.
- She wills him to choose her. The gods intercede. . . .
- Success: he sends her the clandestine note during the last English class (not math, not geography!). Towers exist to be breached, and sympathetic handmaidens exist to carry messages.
- Now she must fight her parents—the king and queen—for permission to see him.
- She primps for hours to become worthy. No self-respecting princess is without a mirror. All interesting characters have flaws, and hers is narcissism.
- When her lover appears, he is summoned for review.

In a plot point, the story abruptly subverts convention. Instead of the handsome but lowly lad being summoned upstairs to appear before the king and queen, the two innocents are summoned by the queen's sepulchral voice from the dungeon. Here she is performing a rite over a recently sacrificed animal. Interrogating the Catch of Barstow, she cuts and scrapes the mink—figuratively cutting and scraping the vulnerable teens.

A slew of ironic *juxtapositions* emerge from my reading of the tale. They include hunter/prey, secret message/English lesson, petitioner/freedom, upper house/lower dungeon, mother/taxidermist, and mink/girl, mink/boy. Narrative art profits from juxtaposing so many opposites, because it confronts the audience with puzzles to solve. Needless to say, the audience performs this work mostly at an unconscious level.

> *Juxtaposition* in narrative art means placing different objects or elements side by side so that the viewer, reader, or listener senses a contrast that requires interpretation. The peace demonstrator who put a flower in a soldier's rifle barrel during a 1960s face-off outside the Pentagon constructed a brilliant paradox. One photo launched a thousand sympathetic press stories, and it has come to symbolize the whole era of unrest. Juxtaposing objects, shots, sounds, or ideas makes the audience search for the implied meaning; it is at the heart of film language.

As aspiring artists, our work is to become familiar with narrative's hidden powers and to become familiar with the tools our forebears have developed.

Amanda's story presents dialectical opposites and archetypal figures, such as king, queen, princess, and handsome but lowly aspiring lover. An irony (and plot point) occurs when the mother/queen, by torturing the young lovers' heightened sensibilities with her sickening hobby, reveals herself as harpie or vampire. Another irony is that it is not "royalty" who holds the ultimate power but the Catch of Barstow. He will take his favors elsewhere. Amanda's family story, by integrating the traditional with the modern, confronts us with elements that make an ironic and eloquent commentary.

These classic techniques of juxtaposition and mythic allusion almost certainly entered the story incrementally, with each retelling. Embellishment is natural; it is how stories grow. Telling, getting feedback, and adjusting the next telling is the oral and theatrical tradition at work, and it has been deliberately incorporated in this book's classroom methods.

Juxtaposition is invaluable, because it can alert the audience to a *subtext*—the underlying will and motivation that one should always seek out beneath the appearance of events in both stories and real life (and see the sidebar). Characters evidence subtexts, but so may a whole scene when it furthers the hidden agenda of the storyteller.

Juxtaposition in film was first called montage, the French word for "showing." According to its Russian theorists, film shots can be edited together according to four principles:

> *Subtexts* are the hidden agendas that one constantly finds in reality and in intelligent fiction. In life we usually protect ourselves by representing our feelings indirectly or misleadingly. A loner neighbor who comes to lend a book may, depending on the context, want to assess your worldly goods, make a new friend, or give an ingratiating impression before the gossips go to work. Scenes of tension usually have subtexts that are ambiguous and at extreme variance with surface events.

- *Structural* (builds the stages of the scene)
- *Relational* (creates contrast, parallels, or symbolism)
- *Conflictual* (counterpoints opposing forces)
- *Elision* (as in a jump cut—field in summer, cut to field covered in snow—indicating a jump forward in time).

Editing is one of several ways to channel spectators' awarenesses and press them into making comparisons. In the writing stage, packing an unfolding situation in the same scene with several characters' viewpoints and indicating several subtextual layers of meaning is favorable, because it needs no intrusive cinema technique like crosscutting to signal its presence. Inventive pictorial composition and blocking (positioning or moving characters and objects within the frame) can produce equally telling juxtapositions, but all within a single frame or shot.

These techniques have their counterparts at the writing stage or in literature. Don't try to use them too consciously in a first draft, or you'll get caught up chasing form when you should concentrate on capturing content. When you come to reread and redraft, your developing eye for dramatic principles will soon find all sorts of vestigial clues waiting to nudge the next stage into being. Writing is an evolutionary process, never a test that you either pass or fail first time.

Example 3 (Peter Riley)

It is 1965 in New York City, the upper West Side on a rainy afternoon, night approaching. The sidewalk is busy with people making their ways home from work, stopping off for a drink, waiting for a bus. An attractive young woman in her early twenties waits at the corner for the light to change, doing her best to cover her hair from the rain with a newspaper.

A fresh-faced man in his early thirties, hair neatly combed and wearing a simple suit, strolls up beside her, his umbrella aloft and shielding him from the drops. He watches the light change and then notices the girl beside him. He is obviously quite taken with her. The crowd on the corner surges across the intersection as the traffic comes to a halt, but he only stands there and watches her walk away. He suddenly snaps to reality and dashes across the corner after her.

The man catches up with the young woman and politely asks her if she'd like to share his umbrella as far as she's going. She is mildly surprised but grateful, and he seems unthreatening. They stroll down the sidewalk and chat about the weather, how the days are getting shorter—until finally the woman stops and announces that she's reached her destination. It seems that she's meeting her boyfriend here for an early dinner. He can be seen waiting at a table inside. The young man, disappointed, tells her it was nice meeting her and carries on his way. She watches him go, curious. Then she enters the restaurant and joins her boyfriend.

As they are about to order, they are suddenly interrupted by the young man with the umbrella, who politely asks the young woman for a moment of her time. She steps into the lobby under the watchful eye of her flustered companion, more curious than ever. The young man presents her with a small bouquet of flowers and tells her he absolutely must see her again.

Author's notes on the story's underlying meaning and importance:

- As romantic and impossible as it may seem, this is how my parents met.

- The story's meaning or importance lies in the chance taken—the fact that a random meeting that could have been only that and nothing more ultimately resulted in a lifetime partnership and a family. Sickening as it may be in our cynical day and age, it is a paean to love at first sight.
- This story presents no real narrative or production problems.
- This story would seem on the surface to have little relation to my themes; but there is a connection to be found with the theme of the individual in the modern world. In this story two souls who are perhaps intended for one another seem to meet by "chance," surrounded by the gloom of the city and its faceless, uninterested inhabitants. The most human of emotions finds its way in an environment that would seem to stamp it out.

Much is happening here. In the brouhaha of the city, rain threatens the mild young woman's beauty and composure, so the chivalrous young man offers to shelter her under his umbrella. This she can accept because, in her coolness and curiosity, she judges him to be nonthreatening. She becomes "more curious than before" when he returns. By presenting the "small bouquet of flowers," he recklessly lets her see his stricken heart and confesses that he "absolutely must see her again." Who could resist such urgent and passionate recognition? The poor boyfriend at the dinner table is nowhere, for all he has to offer is dinner. His rival proffers his heart, improvising gallantry and romance on the spot like some Gene Kelly, singin' in the rain.

Note the confident brevity with which Peter evokes his main character. He "strolls," is "fresh faced," has hair that is "neatly combed," and wears a "simple suit." This detail deftly summons a most appealing image. However, at a later screenplay stage, these adjectives may not be enough. As literary descriptions, their potency may not survive the translation to facts on a screen, where we might need active, behavioral equivalencies that won't be submerged in a busy urban street setting. The audience might easily miss the subtle character-building details of tidy hair and suit. However, what seals the young man's power is reassuringly cinematic. Offering the umbrella against the unfriendly elements, then thrusting the flowers at her with his confession of vulnerability— these are lovely actions, straight from the medieval traditions of courtly love.

If you read the story carefully, you will see that the POV character

> *Character and action descriptions* in a scene outline are best when you use the compressed and evocative language of poetry. But these are for a reader, not the viewer; a camera cannot narrate in the same way. When you get to the screenplay stage, you will need to substitute special shots, actions, and behavior to establish the same values through visual and behavioral means. Ultimately *characters are realized through action,* and we can only infer what they are from what they do.

is Peter's father at the beginning, but that POV migrates to his mother around halfway through.

Young writers often flex their power by creating the dark and the ugly, so it is refreshing to see how Peter honors his parents' qualities and how much he is in love with their love story.

Life has a great deal of beauty for those who seek it: flowers bloom on empty lots, even in New York; love at first sight isn't always a deception; men aren't always dupes or predators; and women aren't always controlling viragos. Good storytellers hold and entertain their audiences by including humor, hope, or gemstone flashes of beauty as leavening to the sterner stuff.

GOING FARTHER

Carmack, Sharon Debartolo. *The Genealogy Sourcebook*. Los Angeles: Lowell House, 1998. (Any good starting guide to genealogy like this will tell you how to start interviewing and logging the details of your family. For obvious reasons, one always starts with the oldest members, one of whom may already be the unofficial family historian. But be warned, you have started down the trail of an addiction!)

Rabiger, Michael. *Directing the Documentary*, 3d ed. Boston: Focal Press 1998. (For more about editing principles, see chapter 5, "Screen Grammar," in particular page 57, "Shots in Juxtaposition.")

Stone, Elizabeth. *Black Sheep and Kissing Cousins: How Our Family Stories Shape Us*. New York: Penguin, 1989. (This is a wide-ranging survey of family stories that, the jacket note says, "define our sense of the unique nature of our families, and our own places in them. They provide us with inspiration, warnings, and cherished values. These stories never leave us; they reverberate through our lives, guiding our choices in work, friendship, and love." This compendium is in three parts, respectively identifying family stories with defining the world, the family, and the individual.)

---9---

A Myth, Legend, or Folktale Retold

The preceding chapters asked you to delve into your inner resources. From now on, you will look outward at other resources awaiting use, but you will be always on the lookout for your own abiding thematic and other interests.

Myths, legends, and folktales are enduring assets that anyone can employ. Indeed, they thrive because they are so adaptable and continue to render useful service. A legend is history made inauthentic from purposeful retelling. That is, the tale treats people who existed and events that actually happened, but in the process of being handed down, the tale has developed in the face of local needs. King Arthur almost certainly existed, but the many variants on the original (or Ur) version show that several European cultures made use of it. The narratives were embellished by countless traveling storytellers over a long period, who adapted them to serve their audiences' changing preoccupations. Now at least a thousand years old, Arthurian legend is still alive and well, and still commenting on love, loyalty, honor, faith,

> *Traditional tales,* such as legends, myths, and folktales are authorless and come to us by oral transmission. All are meant to entertain, which is always the best way to teach. *Legends* are inauthentic history, figures, and events from the past reshaped to serve the special purposes of their tellers. *Myths* are stories usually involving the supernatural, representing the inalterable and often insoluble principles that govern the human condition. *Folktales* are usually cautionary narratives designed to pass on knowledge and outlook that is useful to survival.

humility, and courage—the principles that make life such a test. James Cameron's blockbusting movie *Titanic* (1998) draws deeply from the principles of Arthurian courtly love.

A *myth* is something different. It is a presentational framework, often involving the supernatural, for the aspects of human experience that are inevitable and insoluble. It handles the constants of human experience, which we must swallow, lumps and all. The myth of Narcissus, who drowns from admiring his own image in a pool, is an allegory for the consequences of self-involvement. Rather than propose how to avoid the situation or how to cure egotism, it cheerfully dramatizes the fate of those inattentive to the laws of existence. Myth, by nature fatalistic, inculcates awareness of consequences.

Like legends or myths, *folktales* are also authorless and handed down by oral tradition. Many are concerned with the destiny of the powerless and come to us in the form of ballads or laments. Most, however, are teaching stories, whose job is to impart survival skills. "Little Red Riding Hood" is about the dangers of trusting appearances. The tale of the Signifying Monkey, from Afro-American culture, is about how one can put on a show to manipulate whites by playing up to the stereotypes they hold of blacks.

ASSIGNMENT

Choice of Material

Find a myth, legend, or folktale that you can adapt to a recognizable modern setting. If like most people you have a mixed ethnic makeup, you may find it rather satisfying to research for legends, folktales, or myths among the least familiar aspects of your background. For me this would mean foraging among Celtic and Hispanic tales before resorting to those familiar from my English upbringing.

The material you choose to adapt should appeal to you at a visceral level, rather than merely illustrating your thematic interests. By giving rein to instincts and fascinations one can allow deeper preoccupations to emerge.

Your presentation should include:

1. A short summary of the original tale
2. Your new version written in the usual treatment form
3. A modern setting whose conventions would be credible for a broad audience
4. Believable characters, credibly motivated
5. A plot that doesn't strain credulity.

Be careful that the seductiveness of your tale's moral lesson doesn't blind you to problems of adaptation in a contemporary setting. Many traditional tales hinge upon the effects of a magic potion or upon obedience to archaic customs, such as willing compliance with the dictates of a cruel father. These can severely strain credibility when transferred wholesale to a modern setting.

One could employ "magic realism" and imbue the whole world of the story with magical properties, but the assignment specifically asks for a good tale in a world that runs in the regular way. In the next chapter, where you will be dramatizing dream material, you will be able to construct the most fantastic worlds, running according to the most perverse logic.

The challenge is to find a modern embodiment of an ancient predicament. If your tale calls for a daughter whose obedience is self-destructive, you may have to think hard about where this can be found today (it always can). Maybe you end up specifying an immigrant father whose fundamentalist religion or experience of torture during political imprisonment causes him to make extreme demands on his family. If your story calls for a magic potion, you might solve it by making reckless teenagers take pills at a party, or having an anthropologist drink a shaman's concoction as part of his research. Ingenuity can solve most such problems.

Analysis

Define what your choice of story conveys about:

1. The constants of human behavior
2. The laws of the universe.

EXAMPLES

Example 1: *The Legend of Pretty Boy Floyd Retold* (Michael Hanttula)

A spring night. The wealthy man, P. B. Floyd, driving an expensive sports car, races through the back streets of a suburb, avoiding the police that patrol the main strips. Returning from the shipyard, where he has just completed refinishing the deck of his boat, his tattered jeans and stained shirt desecrate the fine leather seat that they rest on.

Out of the darkness of an alleyway: a blur of spinning red and blue lights angers P. B., and his fist slams against the steering wheel as he pulls his "workday shoe"-covered foot from the accelerator. Pulling over, P. B. begins to prepare the documents that the officer will look for. Reaching for his wallet, P. B. finds an empty pocket and an officer staring down his throat.

He tries to explain, but the officer doesn't trust someone dressed like he is. P. B. is asked to step out of the car—still trying to explain. The officer becomes infuriated with P. B. for attempting to lie his way out of this and calls for backup. P. B. explains that this isn't necessary and the argument heats up. The officer rails at P. B. for insulting his intelligence and barks about his hatred for what criminals like him have done to the city. P. B. continues his attempt to justify himself, but the officer finally replies with a baton to the head. Finding himself on the ground and disoriented, P. B. struggles to stop the officer from beating him. The officer does not relent. As the baton meets his stomach, P. B. is able to grab hold, and he holds on for his life.

The officer becomes even more enraged and threatens him with the consequences as he unleashes his service revolver. Without thought of his action, P. B. pulls forcefully on the baton and then strikes it back in the officer's direction, trying to shake it free. The baton snaps back into the officer's face. With a crack into his nose, the officer's cartilage is forced into his brain, the officer's corpse collapses next to P. B. Sirens are approaching from a mile or so away as P. B. realizes what he has done.

He flees, taking all the money he has with him, into the mountains. Witnesses have described P. B., and he is never able to return to a well-populated area. A slew of crimes following the officer's murder, as well as a few that occurred before (all without suspects), are assumed to have been the work of the malicious P. B. Floyd, who "murdered an officer without thought when pulled over for a routine traffic violation." He is the most feared and hated criminal in the state. He is responsible for more crimes than this region has ever known.

P. B. lives in solitude and almost never makes contact with others, let alone commits any crimes. He does, however, donate what money he can to charities that he used to support when he lived within the good grace of the town, sending only an unmarked packet filled with bills.

The author writes:

I guess this story speaks of mistaken identity. P. B. is never allowed to return because of the identity that the town has given him, so he must leave everything behind and become a hermit—or face conviction and be incarcerated. P. B. is fairly innocent, but witnesses would say that it was he who had attacked the officer. In a police-controlled society, the might of the officer's duty makes what is right: giving the officer the right to act violently, but not the citizen the right to protect him/herself. Once someone is condemned by the state, the people of that state will also condemn that person, feeling as if that person's actions against the state have been made against them personally as well.

A condemned person, when condemned initially, is also likely to be accused as an all-around evil person—whether through accusations of other actual crimes (as in the legend of Pretty Boy Floyd) or in having a criminal mind (so that criminal actions equate with an evil mentality).

As far as my themes are concerned, I seem to deal with stories of misunderstood characters, or the (re)actions that come from misunderstandings. This seems to be a case of wrongful guilt placed upon P. B. that has sentenced him to a lifetime of solitude.

Every story that class members produce will need further development. How to make this happen will usually occupy the class's attention first. In this story, the foreground events need some *backstory* (see the sidebar) to establish local police behavior and the life of the town. Without this, we won't realize that Pretty Boy Floyd is not simply spoiled and resentful by nature but has suffered treatment that justifies his behavior.

After the killing, the narrative would probably have to branch into two stories, told in parallel segments: one following Floyd in his developing solitude, the other showing town life with other crimes being committed that the townspeople ascribe to him in his absence. That he always gave anonymously to charities should also be established early, if the anonymous gifts from his hideout are to have their rightful weight at the movie's end.

Backstory is information about the past that the audience can piece together from clues as a story proceeds. It concerns events and situations that led the story's characters into their present attitudes and situations. *Editorializing* is the sin of making backstory or authorial attitudes emerge blatantly, from "planted" dialogue: "There you are, Alan. And you've just been to visit your father, who bought a share in the mine in 1962."

This story falls under the rubric of "give a dog a bad name," for it illustrates how class or racial stereotyping shackle a person to a troublesome label. Class antagonism on the officer's part seems the cause, because Floyd is good looking and wealthy. He has to be on guard, because the police will harass him. He just wants to get home fast. Pride and irritability are his Achilles' heel, for like Rodney King[1] he won't play the subordinate. Because he lives in a heavily policed society, he must eventually pay for his independence. Killing his tormentor leads inevitably to exile and then to becoming the scapegoat for all unsolved crimes.

We might say "Serves him right," except that in his solitude he still finds ways to relieve the suffering of others. Unlike his precursor Robin Hood, his actions go unknown and unrewarded, and so he more than redeems himself.

---

1. The Los Angeles African-American who refused to stop for a police car and whom the police then beat unmercifully. Amateur videotape coverage triggered an explosive inquiry into police racism and brutality.

Example 2 (Tatsuya Guillermo Ohno)

Southern Japan, a small village. Joshi is a well-known architect and a religious person. He has built numerous churches, all of them in a very traditional style, with a round straight tree placed to support the ceiling at the center of each church. It symbolizes the strength and unity of each believer. A week after he has finished his latest church, the priest tells Joshi that the central tree has a hole and is infected. Leaving the tree in that condition would weaken the tree and the church would fall down. Also the other wood in the church could become infected and become weaker and weaker until it too fell apart. Knowing the dangers, Joshi starts a search party who walk into the middle of the forest.

It is very hot and humid, but the party keeps searching for a tree. They sleep in the forest and the search starts early in the morning. Days go by and they still can't find a tree. Every single one they find is infected and full of holes. Everyone is exhausted but still they keep looking. One night after a week of looking, the search is canceled. First thing in the morning everyone packs to go home, but Joshi doesn't give up and goes on searching for the right tree. The forest is very dark. The moon is the only thing he can see. He can hardly see the trees at all.

Just before dawn he decides to go back but as he returns he bumps into a big, big tree. He is amazed by the size of it, at how perfectly round and straight it is. The sun comes up and he sees that there are no holes in it and that it isn't infected. The search party returns to cut the tree down and with the help of all the villagers the tree is dragged to the village.

The author writes:

The story is about unity. The tree represents unity and in this case the main support. Although the search was exhausting, the entire party worked hard looking for the tree. Hope encouraged Joshi to go on looking one more time for the tree, so the story is also about hope, which is the last thing we have to lose.

This fairly straightforward story, which does not seem quite modern enough to fulfill entirely the assignment, is about faith and persistence. Its hero Joshi is famous for his art and his religiousness, but he has become too comfortable with his success and a little careless. Tatsumo's draft of the story could easily be brushed aside as having an overevident moral. Actually, some vital elements are missing, but they are not hard to find.

You develop an idea by *interrogating* it—that is, by asking all the hard, valid questions that an audience might pose, and by examining the possible answers for their guidance. For instance:

> To *test a plot*, one searches it for implausibilities and omissions. This is done well by a sympathetic group, who become the story's first audience. If the author is to learn all that's possible, he or she must listen carefully to the responses and not leap to defend or explain.

Q: *How does the priest come to report the tree's failure to Joshi?*
A: Maybe with pain and disbelief, suggesting that the new church is literally rotten at the core and Joshi must rectify the disaster.

Q: *How does Joshi react?*
A: Perhaps at first with anger and disbelief, until he sees that his work is indeed faulty. It is always useful to make a character's path more difficult and to build resistance and tension into situations. Such resistance can be internal or external.

Q: *How does Joshi atone for his mistake?*
A: Maybe after seeing that he has truly failed, he must overcome his pride and accept that he failed because he had become overconfident in his powers. Dramatically speaking, this prepares the way for a moral epiphany of considerable dimension.

Q: *How does he tell the villagers?*
A: The villagers might already know from the priest, or the priest could offer to tell them on Joshi's behalf, but it would be more powerful if Joshi took it upon himself to tell them. This would be a path of self-inflicted humility that he chooses to follow. This is called "raising the stakes."

> *Raising the stakes.* Whenever you find ways to intensify a character's obstacles, you make that character "play for higher stakes." This engenders a stronger dramatic experience, because the character must struggle harder. Conflict and the struggle to do or get are at the heart of drama.

Q: *How does he get the villagers to follow him into the forest?*
A: Perhaps they first make him go to search alone; failing, he has to return humbly to ask for their support.

Q: *How does Joshi keep the villagers going when the forest yields only rotten trees?*
A: This is a chance to develop Joshi's internal and external conflict as he faces the biggest crisis of his career. He might even go through a crisis of belief, as Christ does upon the cross when he asks, "Father why hast thou forsaken me?"

Q: *Are all the villagers to remain undifferentiated?*
A: This degree of abstraction is both possible and even desirable in a

literary form, but it is difficult in film, where it is impractical to conceal that there are different types and ages. In any case, it would make for a richer story if among the villagers there were doubters as well as believers. Then Joshi would have both helpers and hinderers to lead, a dramatically richer mix.

Q: *Where is God when Joshi, who thinks he has paid his dues as a worshiper, needs him?*

A: Joshi as the main character will eventually put his faults away and prove himself a hero. But heroes aren't heroes unless severely tested. Christ's disciples deserted him in his hour of greatest need; he had to overcome the final test alone.

By applying the conventions that go with a type of story, and by asking a series of natural questions, a host of developmental possibilities begin to appear. Depending on taste, an author can either fulfill an audience's expectations or go some way along a path only to veer off unexpectedly in another direction

> *Genre* refers to types of story or artwork. Romantic comedy, documentary, and *film noir* are well known screen genres; blues, hard rock, symphonies, and jazz are genres of music.

at a plot point. The name given to classes of story is *genre*, the French word for type or class. The labels of buddy story, comedy *noir*, Westerns, historical romance, biography, epic, melodrama, or sci-fi all bring audience expectations that are useful.

A known genre not only provides a degree of shorthand but also provides well-loved structures and suggests aesthetic elements, like tone and lighting. Using genre draws on a common language that helps to communicate the story. The world a genre promises even helps to draw in the right audience.

A genre also limits what you can do, but not unreasonably. While you don't expect to see a goofy cartoon cat stroll into a biblical epic, it is often permissible to combine or subvert genres. Indeed, though we gravitate toward what we like, we also hope that it contains something revolutionary.

Film critics wearied by the repetition of formulae are excellent at genre spotting; the film industry trade paper *Variety* has raised ironic pigeonholing to a veritable art form. Since artists and audiences alike hunger for the new, genres are forced to undergo evolutionary modification.

Example 3: *Sisyphus Cries Dixie: A Modern Story* (Michelle Arnove)

On a deserted street just off the center of town in New Orleans, lies a beat up, half-burned-down building. Echoes from the Mardi Gras celebration going on a few blocks away shake the tattered stairs and walls of 10 Stone Hill Street. Three men occupy a room on the tired fourth floor. Two of them stand stiffly next to either side of the door. A large, well manicured man named Æsopus sits center floor in a large chair behind a wooden table. Sisyphus, a muscular man in his early '20s enters the room and sits on the end of the table with great confidence.

Æsopus, a formidable father figure to the "crawfish cavalry"—a local money laundering group—explains his family plight to Sisyphus. His daughter Ægina has eloped with Jupiter, a man known as a bad news gambler about town. Sisyphus is a freelance journalist and is married to Harouka, the daughter of an extremely wealthy Arabian prince. Since Sisyphus belongs to the country club and socializes with many in these circles, Æsopus thinks that Sisyphus might have information on his daughter's whereabouts. He thinks she was taken against her will and offers to compensate Sisyphus in exchange for the facts. Æsopus does not want to go to the local police due to his long-standing judicial differences of opinion over criminal operations. Lacking no wealth, Sisyphus prefers to be given a bottle of vintage wine from Æsopus's infamous wine cellar. Æsopus agrees to this but warns Sisyphus of pitfalls in the situation.

Since he has entrusted Sisyphus with his daughter's plight, Sisyphus "must come through or else." "Or else what?" responds Sisyphus. Æsopus will send his main man after him—Pluto, who runs Æsopus's bottle-capping company. A factory down in the lower end of town, the company is a sorry excuse for an encapsulated sweat shop. As it turns out, Pluto's top man, whom they call Death, has been in the hospital due to a golf cart accident with Sisyphus. They had been playing a round of golf, and Death was ahead in his game but fell from the golf cart on the way to the next hole. Word had it that Sisyphus, angry that he might lose, pushed Death from the cart as they were cruising at top speed across the putting green. Death ended up with a broken arm, broken leg, and fractured vertebrae. Pluto is not happy about this incident.

Æsopus makes an agreement with Sisyphus that if he does not capture Jupiter and Ægina and bring them back to good ole' New Orleans, Sisyphus will have to go to work for Æsopus under Pluto. The deal is on . . . until time runs out. Sisyphus tells his wife of the arrangement he made with Æsopus. He asks her to contact her father to help him out. Disgusted with Sisyphus's continuous trouble-making schemes, the wife runs away with Pluto's cousin, Erilias.

Sisyphus fails and has no choice but to go to work for Æsopus under Pluto's command.

After a week at the factory in the posh back offices, Sisyphus cons Pluto into letting him off for a few days to find his wife and Erilias. He heads for the country club first, and finds himself engaged in a round of golf three hours later. His friends, happy to see him, drag him out first to dinner and later to a dance club. One of his friends, Olympus, offers him a job as caretaker on his private island and offers keys to the estate and all its treasures. Sisyphus, without hesitation, snatches the opportunity.

Three years later, as he lounges on the empty beach, a yacht bearing Æsopus and Pluto arrives nearby. At gunpoint, they take Sisyphus back to the States.

The factory, now more run-down than ever, continues to manufacture bottles and caps. Sisyphus is demoted from his previous posh position under Pluto to low man on the bottle-capping assembly line. Here the bottles never stop lining up and the bins of caps runneth over.

Every evening, Sisyphus is taken to a dorm-style room and is watched over by Pluto's security guards. This is his destiny . . . to be forevermore a bottle capper.

The author writes:

As I could never come close to the original magical *Myth of Sisyphus*, understanding Camus's reflective comment on how human beings are the masters of their own fate is somewhat complex. However, I will give it a try.

The original myth points to a number of notions about humankind and destiny. First, I would say that Camus is trying to point out that we are responsible for our own actions and bring about our own destiny through indirect self-deprecating actions. In other words, sometimes we take for granted what we have and then must test the truth of its existence, losing in the process. Sisyphus had all that he needed, but was tempted with more. When he tested his possessions, he lost all that he enjoyed. Given an opportunity for redemption, he once again tested his ownership of his goods and ended up far worse off.

The other defining point of the myth is the notion of repetition and counter-progression as a living hell. Maybe my own beliefs in variety, growth, and progression as the primary needs for happiness in life leave me with the feeling that destitution and "hell," as we'd have it, is doing the same thing, day in and day out, with no satisfactory outcome. To spend one's life doing meaningless, menial, laborious activities and never seeing any change or growth, either in oneself or the objects of one's focus, equates to nothingness, especially when one's life is ruled by another person and choices are not elements in the equation.

The setting—Mafia types in a run-down New Orleans setting—is replete with atmospheric possibility. It is a male-dominated world where wives, girlfriends, and daughters are property. The godfather (like his namesake) deals out assignments that may garner promotion or punishment. Condemning Sisyphus to do menial factory ever after is the author's highly workable parallel to the mythical figure's punishment. Sisyphus fails from overconfidence and inattention to the dangers of his task.

I only wish the author had substituted modern names, as the ancient ones keep me from sinking completely into the story. However, we do have a good beginning and a good ending (Sisyphus drearily capping bottles for eternity). Since this is Sisyphus's fate, it would be nice to make him see, when first entering the situation as a confident young journalist, something or someone that foreshadows his destiny.

Myths often reverse our expectations. Since Sisyphus is the hero, we expect him to win. But the story has a sting in its tail, and by making him fail, it focuses our attention on the vulnerabilities underlying his failure.

The outline has a couple of missing links. Why does Sisyphus fail to find Ægina? How does Æsopus's wife become pivotal to Sisyphus's failure? In the original myth, Zeus has Æsopus's daughter taken away by an eagle. Sisyphus happens to see the abduction and makes the tactical mistake of snitching on Zeus, who consigns him to rolling his rock eternally uphill. Because of this he fails to help the dispossessed father. The chain of causality would need mending for the next draft.

DISCUSSION

Novalis said that "character is destiny." All the above adaptations—from an American legend, from a Japanese folktale, and from a Greek myth—deal with characters whose fates pivot on their innate qualities. Joshi, after truly signifying humility, triumphs; Pretty Boy is outlawed but keeps his humanity; while Sisyphus is consigned to dehumanizing toil. As you make your bed, so do you lie.

We are perennially interested in what makes characters tick, what they do to merit good or bad fortune, and what influences the system of justice meted out by providence. Civilization depends on people of good will acting for the benefit of the majority. Many stories discuss this by showing what a person must do to become a leader instead of barely surviving, down among the dead men. Two of our characters merely survive, because they make bad judgments, overestimate their abilities, or otherwise fail to adapt to reality.

One (Joshi) sees reality but refuses to accept that God really wants to see him defeated, so he goes on searching. That his faith and persistence are ultimately rewarded is the message to the villagers and to us.

What is truly fascinating is that each of our three authors (unknowingly, I think) tells a story that enacts what folklorist Joseph Campbell asserted: that a common structure lies behind many a hero or heroine's journey, no matter where or when the story originates. Campbell's *Hero with a Thousand Faces* shows that in the archetypical trajectory:

> The *Hero's Journey* is what the folklorist Joseph Campbell calls the paradigm he found behind so many of the world's stock of folktales. Hollywood covered the same ground by studying audiences and box office receipts.

- The hero is first seen in a familiar world.
- He receives a call to the mission or action.
- He may first refuse the call.
- The call comes in a more urgent and ineluctable form.
- Accepting the call, the hero passes into an unfamiliar world
- Along the way toward his mission, he faces a series of increasingly severe tests of courage, ingenuity, persistence, faith, etc.
- During these tests he meets a variety of helpers and hinderers—allies, counselors, tricksters, and enemies—as things get more difficult.
- There is often a mentor from whom to learn.
- Approaching the inmost cave, he faces the supreme test.
- Here, at the supreme test, the hero may win or lose.
- If he wins, he gets the supreme reward (often the elixir of knowledge).
- Resurrection—tested and strengthened, and bearing the elixir of knowledge, he returns to the normal world.

By tracking audience tastes, Hollywood's immigrant moguls quickly discovered the strength and durability of traditional forms. A thousand or more years earlier, the troubadours and companies of roving actors must have made similar findings, by a similar process. In our work together we will often apply what they can teach us, for in such an expensive medium as film it would be folly to reject such proven wisdom out of hand. This need not lead to stale or formulaic storytelling, since there are vast numbers of new characters and settings awaiting your use.

GOING FARTHER

Caution: use this book to assist in rethinking something you have already written, never as a starting point for a new idea. Otherwise, you risk paralysis from trying to write within a constricting plan.

Vogler, Christopher. *The Writer's Journey: Mythic Structure for Storytellers and Screenwriters*. Studio City, CA: Michael Wiese Productions, 1992. (This work shows how closely Campbell's paradigm fits not only Dorothy's career in *The Wizard of Oz* but that of hundreds of other screen heroes and heroines.)

——————10——————
Dream Story

The work in this chapter invites you to break completely with a major writing enemy—over-control. Of course, your writing should never lack control, but in the early stages a piece can easily be destroyed by trying to follow patterns instilled in earlier life. Remember in high school, facing a blank sheet of paper and trying to get started with the approved essay process? Hating the rigidity of the process, and already bored with the subject matter, we tried to knock it off in one pass, like swallowing bitter medicine.

Writing is a two-part process. First generate new material fast and intuitively, so you can keep up with your mind's inventions. Second, edit, using your powers of analysis and restructuring. Try never to wear both hats at once, as it leads to self-censorship and even paralysis.

Too much structure, too many rules too early, block the mind's ability to draw on its deepest levels of observation and comprehension. First drafts need to be written as they come to mind, with no other thought than to get it all down on paper. To do otherwise is to labor under a crippling self-consciousness. Write first in private, and write with utter freedom. Afterward, put on your story-editing hat and find a better order for your free-running mind's output. You will be surprised at how much order and thought-provoking substance already exists.

We can only see what the mind can produce when it is freed of all self-censorship, and this is only completely true when one is asleep and dreaming.

Being true to the distinctive logic of dream is a rehearsal for being true to the way things often happen in life, which seldom happens as we imagine. What most people call imagination is really a memory stuffed with clichés. Evict these stereotypes by studying closely the profundity of the actual.

ASSIGNMENT

Writing Up a Dream

The assignment is to use the material of a dream (or dreams) and, most importantly, to preserve dreaming's weird logic. You will be surprised at what's waiting for you there. So, from the journal of dreams that you have been keeping:

1. Write a treatment for a story that might last, say, five minutes on screen. It could be one long dream or several fragments ingeniously joined together.
2. Do not worry about a tidy beginning or ending, or about conventional story logic. Instead, be as faithful as possible to the mood and logic of dream itself.
3. You are free to alter or augment in order to serve the spirit of the dream world.

Analysis

Define what themes or messages the story seems to be developing.

EXAMPLES

Dream Sequence #1 (Chris Darner)

An average-looking man in unassuming clothing is led along a path, carved into a sheer sea cliff. In front of him a short, crooked man keeps up a brisk pace. The average man slows and sputters in his walk, staring out at the vastness of everything around him. Below the two travelers is a deep-green ocean, its waves crashing up far below them, a salty white mist rising into the air. The two continue on the narrow trail, the crooked man constantly pulling and tugging at the average man. The path bends up ahead and the crooked man pulls more eagerly than ever, increasing the pace to a near jog.

As the path curves around the cliff, land comes into view—lush tropical vegetation and a white-sand beach. The average man scans the new view and his pace slows. The crooked man doesn't notice, however, and continues on his brisk pace, leaving the average man slowly drifting farther behind. The average man continues his scanning, stumbling along the trail. His eyes catch a small raft floating down below in the sea.

He holds up his hand to shade his eyes and help him focus in the bright light. Slowly the image comes into focus. There are two brothers frolicking in the water. They both look very similar and could very likely be twins. They have plain, muted features, appear to be about 25 years old and are extremely obese. Wearing nothing but small bathing suits, their bodies resemble white walruses, their flesh rippling with every movement. The average man can hear faint echoes of their laughing and giggling mixed with the sounds of the crashing waves still below him. The two brothers chuckle and chortle, playing in and around the raft. They take turns pulling their massive frames up into their small boat and then falling back off the side of the raft, which folds and stresses under their weight. The average man sits there stunned, his movement along the path having halted seconds into the observation.

The crooked man returns and curtly pulls at the average man, though not out of spite. The average man stumbles along the path, once again following the crooked man. He glances back one last time, hears the twins playing on the raft, then twists around to follow the crooked man, who is leading as eagerly as ever.

The author writes:

This dream sequence seems to develop upon a theme outside of my current theme list but does touch upon one. The main theme of the piece is alienation and being somewhere intimidating and foreign. The crooked man pulls the average man along, because he is either unable to maneuver in the unfamiliar territory, or is hesitant. When the average man sees the brothers he stops and watches them. While I didn't write in his internal reactions to the situation, they hopefully read as uncomfortable, and that he somehow feels it is indecent. This response, and anywhere you are uncomfortable with people around you, does touch partially on my theme of fear of either being or becoming that which you hate. In other words, the average man sees something in the brothers that he sees, or could see, in himself.

My themes have been finding their way into my writings, both inside of class and out, fairly consistently. One theme that I do notice in my writings is alienation and a feeling of being somewhere forbidden or taboo. This dream sequence illustrates that fairly well.

Although its imagery is rendered quite minimally, the visual texture of this dream is stark and vivid. Of the four characters, three are physically deformed. The crooked man is the average man's guide, a sort of stunted Father Time, bustling their shared journey forward. He is wholly focused on the purpose of the journey, while the average man wants to linger and gaze around him. As he takes in the natural and beautifully evoked seascape, his gaze is captured by the two fat, white walrus boys. Their play is repulsively fascinating, and he goes on watching voyeuristically until chivvied by his guide. These twin souls are a phenomenon that he feels he must not dwell upon, yet he cannot help looking back at them over his shoulder as the crooked man tugs him onward. From the author's notes, the average man seems to be witnessing his own worst fate—pale obesity with only himself for companionship.

Dream Sequence #2: *To Torture an "Artiste"* (Louis Leterrier)

A red Pinto with a *Starsky and Hutch* white stripe on its side pulls out in the middle of the Villa Borghese in Roma, Italy, where Pierre, a French poet, is boring a crowd of young beautiful Swedish female teenagers with the verses he wrote the night before, zealous because of the five cappuccinos he has ingested. Two middle-aged men come out of the vehicle, their faces covered by discolored pantyhose. Their guts flab away from their wife-beater tank-tops as they run across the square and jump on Pierre, trapping him inside a potato bag. They drag his motionless body inside the car.

It's dark inside the bag but Pierre isn't scared, he is trying to philosophize about the situation by speaking to himself in his native language. "Shut your big yapper!" screams the driver, with a heavy Midwest accent. Pierre does so. He understands English but refuses to use it; French is so perfect a tongue that no other language is necessary. A vague yet intense smell of B.O., bad beer, or urine fills the air.

When the two men remove the bag from Pierre's head he finds himself in the common room of a trailer. He looks out of the window where other Winnebagos are gathered. It's a trailer park, probably in South Carolina. Pierre has heard about this monstrous concept but could never have imagined intentionally visiting one. He starts sweating bullets. His foundation melts on his black turtle neck.

One of the men enters the room pulling something behind him. It's an old TV set. He positions it in front of Pierre. Then he takes the pantyhose off his head. The man is rather short and stocky, and his five o'clock shadow makes a horrible sound when rubbed against the stocking. His dirty blond hair is cut very short on top, a crew cut, but the man lets his greasy hair grow long in the back. Pierre looks at him intensively, although he is disgusted by his appearance, but doesn't recognize him. The man turns the TV set on and sits next to Pierre, who's tied to an armchair protected by a clear plastic cover. The man starts switching channels in no particular order looking for the most horrific programs he can find—afternoon talk shows, paranormal shows, soap operas etc.

The other man sits down on the other side of Pierre, who starts to feel extremely ill at ease. He has brought a huge bag of potato chips with him. He tears the bag open, and as the artificial BBQ flavor fills the room, Pierre gags. Then the second man puts a twelve-pack of Budweiser on Pierre's lap. The two men grab a beer can each and open them. The warm foam splatters Jim's anthracite wool sports jacket from Agnes B.

One hours, two hours, the whole day passes by, and Pierre, to whom they've been feeding all this junk for the entire day, finishes by fainting.

The Pinto whizzes by the Champs de Mars in Paris. The passenger door opens and Pierre's lifeless body rolls on to the sidewalk. A Parisian crowd gathered at the terrace of a café screams before surrounding the body. A note on his chest reads: "Let this be an example, artistes!"

The author writes:

> This dream is true, nothing in it has been invented. As twisted as it seems I dreamt this story a few weeks ago, that's why I'm not sure I can find one of my themes. Those that are presented are: paranoia about what you don't know; and the clash of the classes. More than being strictly racial or economic, these clashes are intellectual. I don't know which of the two extremes I would rather belong to.

The dream seems to dramatize several forces that the author feels opposed in his identity—French versus American, highbrow versus lowbrow, urbanite versus rural redneck. The story brings all these under the cynical magnifying glass of comedy, evoking a range of discomforts and lampooning his own least-favorite people, the central one being a self-figure.

> *Dreams* send important but coded messages to the dreamer. They conduct a tireless campaign to entertain, educate, and advise their host. Study yours and you'll find a fund of ideas and opinions that you didn't know you owned.

Pierre is abducted for his pretensions, exposed by philistines to the intellectual torture of American daytime TV, then returned dead to his Parisian origins as a warning to his effete café accomplices. Unmistakably the language is that of satire, a form where prevailing vices are held up for ridicule, a clash of caricatured opposites.

In France, deriding highbrow pretensions is in the tradition of Moliere, Voltaire, and more recently Jacques Tati. American exponents are Mark Twain, Flannery O'Connor, and Woody Allen, to mention but a few.

Dreams inform us of our thematic preoccupations, and sometimes they suggest a genre or form of presentation that is specific to the subject matter. Louis's dream is an ironic mirror that casts strong doubt on the validity of his arty aspirations. It metes out an equally caustic critique of the America in which Pierre finds himself by making it into a theater of the absurd. Evidently Louis's dreaming mind considers that a bracing dose of self-mockery will be good for his ego.

Dream Sequence #3 (Michael Hanttula)

An immaculately clear sky, radiant blue. Tall grass that has been worn to a light brown by the beaming sun sways playfully in the cool breeze. A trail stretches far across this land, snuggled between a long body of water and rolling hills. It is absolutely quiet, except for the grasses, which seem to snicker as they rub against each other. There is a group of young men hiking along this mountainous trail. The sun is beating down on them, browning them like the grass, and the calm expanse of the dark lake beckons them to divert their path. They pause and contemplate a swim when their attention is stolen by a curious crack in an enormous boulder behind them.

One of the men investigates the crack, which is formed by a large stone plate that seems to be slowly dismembering itself from the larger portion of rock. Behind this plate, the man finds a small opening that leads inside the boulder. The rest of the group, increasingly curious, join the young man.

> *Character archetypes*, more symbolic than individualized, often appear in dreams. They are either hardwired in our genetics or inculcated through our culture. *Narrative structural archetypes* also seem inherent to our minds. How else could dreams, which usually seem so fragmentary and random, so perfectly exemplify a narrative tradition once in a while?

They cautiously creep inside this enormous rock to find a stone-walled room, with an abundance of ceiling height for what it lacks in floor space. It could have been an antechamber to a medium-sized pyramid. There is a large stone statue of an indiscernible figure standing before them, draped in a dark gray and black linen; it watches them, it watches who enters. A dark tunnel streams off to the right; it is not very inviting. They find the lengthy doorway-like hole to the left of the figure much more appealing.

In a bit of a nervous fright over a possible forthcoming adventure, they scurry through the length of the "doorway." Three enormous stone slabs slam down behind them— meant to trap them individually. Now in a new room, they find a large pit taking up a good area of the floor before them. Its depth is unknown, for it beams an intense light upward. The high ceiling is surprisingly dark given the intensity of the light. Returning from the heights of the ceiling down the length of the near wall are three gigantic stained-glass windows with gothic arches and no particular design, yet apparently medieval. On the ground, the group discovers a plenitude of odd-shaped stones. Some resemble religious objects—crosses and ankhs. The friends decide that they have had enough of this adventure and pick up the stones to beat out the stained glass windows. One of the windows "pops" out of its molding and slips outward. The ground below is now a few hundred feet down. Looking out of this new portal, they see old-growth redwoods that have grown past the height of their view. This exit is not an option.

Turning back toward the room, they see a small ledge on one side of the gleaming crater. They shimmy their way across to the other side, fearful of plummeting to its possible depths. As they reach the other side, they are met by a small cliff (of about three feet or so) that is topped with a fairly severe incline. The only way out seems farther within. They attempt to climb this subterranean hill but find that its composition is of such loose dirt that their arms are buried to the shoulders by the time they can manage a grip. Just as it seems impossible, one of the group discovers another way out, a passage to the right side. They hurry through the tunnel and find themselves landing on the edge of a pool.

A white-bottomed pool with bright lights illuminating it, one you might find in a suburban residence, yet underground. Floating in the pool are dozens of severed human appendages, mostly full arms and legs. Yet the pool's water is clear. One of the boys jumps in and swims safely to the other side. Following his lead, the others jump in. Just as they do, a large dragon's head that the boys hadn't seen before emerges from a far side of this medium-sized pool. It's red, with fiery eyes, made from durable plastic. One may have seen its like at an amusement park. Opening its mouth to toast the group with flames, it coats the clustering youths with a fine watery spray. They hop out of the pool, happy to be alive and beaming with adrenaline.

The room continues on one side, apparently naturally formed pillars leading off into the darkness. However, on the other side is the tunnel they had seen before in the antechamber. They rush through it, laughing at the statue as they make their way out the boulder's entrance. Enraged by their lack of respect, the statue transforms into a human, shielded by a box over her head, and chases them away.

The author writes:

It's rather difficult to find any overwhelming themes or direct purpose to this dream, but it does seem to deal with adventure, religion, mortality, and the bond between friends. Odd, because this was a recurring dream that I once had with each new set of friends, and have not had since the last time that I had a unified "group" of friends.

It seems as if my interests, thematically speaking, have been expanded to also include: the loss of innocence, alienation, and the conflict of wanting to "do good" in a corrupt environment.

This dream was written out as one big, formless paragraph; I have taken the liberty of inserting paragraph breaks. This makes it easier to read, but also indicates some vital shifts between its stages. For this astonishing dream is a textbook example of the hero's journey and its symbols. It could have been composed by Carl Jung and Joseph Campbell working together with a dramaturg. Dreams are usually fragmentary and illogical, but close analysis shows a fascinating structure to this one. Consider:

Act I
- The sunburned young gods amid the trail/sun/water/hills of normal life.
- The call to adventure in the cracked rock with its passageway leading into the hill.
- The first chamber guarded by the draped stone figure.

Act II
- A one-way passage leading to the second chamber containing religious symbols/church windows/blinding light from (hell?) below.

- From here, there are at first two blocked routes of escape.
- But a third way leads to the third and inmost cavern.
- Escape from the inner cave is only possible by the supreme test—confronting horror by passing through the pool of severed limbs.

Act III

- Finally they must run the gauntlet of the statue that comes to life, an enraged maternal female that chases them blindfold, like the figure of Justice.

> The *three-act structure*, though not ubiquitous, is very common in Western drama. It offers a useful way of dividing any story into fundamental stages:
> *Act I* establishes the characters, relationships, and situation, and it defines the dominant problem that the main character confronts.
> *Act II* develops the complications in relationships and situations as the main character struggles with the obstacles that prevent the solving of his/her main problem.
> *Act III* intensifies the situation and resolves it, often in a climactic way that is emotionally satisfying.

For the band of friends, the lightly undertaken journey into the hill, with its three caverns, and back is a supreme test of endurance, courage, and collaborative inventiveness. Facing the terror and mysteries of the journey and emerging unharmed through cooperation and ingenuity, they seem to epitomize the value of teamwork.

Interestingly, the dream is less an individual hero's journey than a collective or even generational rite of passage into manhood. Michael reports having repeatedly experienced this dream with each new group he has joined, as though his mind has to calm his insecurities by repeating the tale. Other elements in the dream suggest preoccupations that only he could decipher, such as the veiled female guardian and the pool of severed limbs.

Dream Sequence #4 (Cynthia Merwarth)

Her arms are full of the day's worth of shopping. As she walks up to the mall exit the guard unlocks the door and lets her out. Time must have flown by because the mall seemed full to her when she was in the stores. But now the parking lot is strangely deserted—all except for her car, which looks as though it is miles away (farther than she remembered having parked it).

It is dark and the parking lot lights illuminate the barrenness. As she walks to her car she hears the sound of growling. Turning, she sees a pack of wild dogs coming for her at a rapid pace. The car seems so far away, but she runs quickly. The growling sounds are closer, louder, more imminent. She runs forever, always hearing the sounds of the dogs behind her. She fumbles with her keys—that particular sound seems so loud and long. The car door flies open and she tries to get in, but as she is shutting the door a dog rips at her heel, making her scream in pain. She kicks it away and slams the door shut.

Now the pack of dogs howl and encircle the car in a predatory rhythmic dance—as if they were going around a fire. Time stands still as she honks the horn again and again, trying to rouse some sign of life in the empty lot.

She is now driving and the dogs are running behind her, never losing sight of her. She can see them in the rearview mirror. The road is dirt. It is deserted. She comes to a gas station and runs out of her car looking for help.

As she runs up to the station attendant he swipes at her with his hand and tells her to "get out of here." He gestures to hit her and stomps his feet at her. She backs off, not believing his refusal to listen to what she has just been through. She is trying to tell him as fast as possible and all he is doing is running from her and trying to hit her. As she runs past an aluminum wall of the building—following the attendant—she catches a glimpse of a wild dog near her. She freezes with terror. The dog is sitting and proceeds to tell her that the man will not help her . . . that the man cannot understand her.

Why can she understand the dog? She thinks . . . It's talking! She sees another dog in the reflection of the aluminum, where her reflection should be! She has become one of the dogs of the night.

The author writes:

> The theme that seems to be developing here is "fear of the unknown," and the realization that I am just like what scares me most. Suffering, death, and violence are all a part of the thematic content in this dream. Also, wanting answers to things that cannot be answered and the frustration and fear that goes along with that feeling.

Although the journey here is quite short in duration, it also follows a similar three act evolution:

Act I

- The journey begins in the safe, normal, and sheltered world of the shopping mall.

- The gatekeeper closes the door behind her so she cannot return.
- She faces the changed world of the nighttime parking lot.

Act II

- To get to the haven of her car she must evade the "wolf" pack, which wounds her (Achilles'?) heel and nearly gets her.
- When she finds a sanctuary, a helper rejects her needs as though she were a fleeing Jew in Nazi dominated Europe.
- The dogs, now more plainly her demons, have caught up with her again.

Act III

- Expecting to be devoured she finds that one dog talks to her and helps her. Though her own species rejects her, an enemy reveals himself a friend and mentor. Can she trust him?
- In reality's mirror she finds that she has involuntarily joined the enemy by becoming one of them.

Among the archetypes here—gatekeeper, fleeing victim, pursuing demons, a potential savior who washes his hands of her—there are three appearances by *shapeshifters*, protean figures who appear in one guise but turn into another. The garage attendant is one, the talking dog the second. The third is the main character herself, who discovers in the mirror that she has changed into "one of the dogs of the night."

Shapeshifters, according to Vogler[1] are often catalysts for change. But the garage attendant betrays his responsibilities and sends her out into the night. In another reversal, the dog that came to devour her turns into her mentor (another archetype), advising her that the man cannot understand her. In the mirror of the garage's polished wall she sees herself next to her fearsome canine guide and understands that she is a dog, that she belongs with the outcast creatures rather than mankind. This is why the man tried to evict her.

Analyze the dream, not the dreamer. The separation can be a fine line, but the dream is a narrative tale, while the dreamer is a person. Unless you are a trained specialist, analyzing the dreamer is likely to be intrusive and objectionable to the author, who will feel forced into self-exposure.

I find the ending both moving and ambiguous. It is hopeful, because she has found the sanctuary of a calm adviser, but she knows that she has become what she most fears. To go any farther would be to second-guess what the symbols mean to the writer, and we have pledged to search for story materials, not psychoanalyze writers.

1. Vogler, Christopher. *The Writer's Journey*. Laurel Canyon, CA: Michael Wiese Productions, 1992:77.

DISCUSSION

Dreams are often incredibly cinematic and at the same time rich with structural and symbolic possibilities. The experience of seeing a good film has often been likened to dreaming. The Surrealist genre of painting and filmmaking in the 1920s and 1930s, like Expressionism in painting and other arts of that period, understood how often human narratives are rooted deep in the turmoil and conflicts of the individual psyche. They saw that being asleep and dreaming was not so different

> Dreams offer an analysis in story, symbolic, and metaphoric form of the chaotic, surreal experience we call our waking life.

from being awake and fully experiencing life, subjectively. Surrealism was expressly interested in the dream world and dream "illogic," which finally is not illogical at all but philosophical in span and metaphorical in language.

The transcribed dreams in your dream journal will probably show principles important to anyone working in the arts, namely that:

- Emotionally loaded narrative is often sparse, visual, and nonliteral. This offers an open framework that invites the audience to decompress it, recreating what the narrative implies but withholds. (You can understand the importance of *withholding* if you watch a bad soap opera.

> *Withholding information* is a valuable way to delay closure and thus maintain tension. Delay answering your audience's questions as long as possible. Profound messages usually make us work to get their meaning. We don't forget what we worked hard to attain.

  It verbalizes and completes every aspect of the story, sapping the viewer of choices or active judgment).

- Vital elements can be juxtaposed in ways that at first seem irrational and confusing but subsequently prove to be only nonlinear. This puts tension and tone ahead of intellectual logic. This is more subjective, and it accurately mirrors how we experience very pressured situations. As an option for narrative mood and structure, it's true to the audience's experience, and it makes a good choice.

- What we do not work for, we do not value. Profound messages, as in Shakespeare's sonnets, demand interpretive work. Like the occasional film that isn't afraid to be densely layered with meaning,[2] dreams and poetry require that we ponder their ambiguities until the point where we *penetrate and remember* their meanings.

2. See Wim Wenders's two masterpieces about the Berlin angels who listen in to human lives and long to join them, *Wings of Desire* (1988) and *Faraway, So Close* (1993).

- By default, dialogue that is only a line or two in an otherwise unbroken flow of action raises the value of language. Dialogue that is spendthrift debases itself.
- Your dreams, though free, will never be easy. Record them over a period of months or years, and slowly your true thematic preoccupations will emerge, along with your demons, archetypes, and unfinished business in life. What more could a storyteller ask?

GOING FARTHER

Buñuel, Luis. *My Last Sigh.* New York: Vintage Books, 1984. (The father of cinema surrealism, whose films continue to galvanize audiences of young and old into a state of shock and excitement, writes candidly about his development—from being boyhood in provincial Spain, to his involvement with the great surrealist painters, writers, and filmmakers in Paris. He went on to make some of the most contentious and dreamlike films of the century.)

Koch-Sheras, Phyllis, and Amy Lemley. *The Dream Sourcebook: A Guide to the Theory and Interpretation of Dreams.* Los Angeles: Contemporary Books, 1995/6. (A cultural and physiological history of dreams and dreaming that instructs on recall techniques. Introduces the more and less famous theorists of dream, and discusses dream symbolism. Classifies dreams as: message; healing; problem solving and creative; mystical, visionary or "high"; completion; recurring; and lucid [where the dreamer is aware of dreaming]).

Jung, Carl. *Man and His Symbols.* Garden City, NY: Doubleday, 1983. (Jung is famous for positing the idea of a collective unconscious, and his work dovetails with Joseph Campbell's in distinguishing what is innate to mankind and thus culturally universal.)

---11---

Adapting a Short Story

If you intend to make a screen version of another person's work, you must first get written permission from the author or the author's literary estate. The exception is when the work is old enough to be in the public domain. Deciding what is old enough can be tricky, as public property in one country may be copyrighted work in another, and this would leave you unable to show your film internationally.

However, this is looking too far ahead. The purpose here is to select and discuss published short stories, not turn them into films. This chapter's goals are to have you:

- Sample the delights of the short-story form.
- Search for a tale that is visual and cinematic.
- Assess what may pose special problems in adaptation.
- Locate a tale dealing with a world and themes to which you strongly resonate.

As you read around, you will find yourself having to resist the seductions that good literature practices on the reader. Will this story work well through image and action on the screen, or does it depend on more interior or literary means? No written story is utterly untranslatable to the screen, but many pose so many difficulties that the effort would be misplaced. That

Making an adaptation. Each medium has its own strengths and weaknesses, and for this reason "faithful" adaptations from literature to film tend to miscarry. Avoid being over-reverent toward the original and think hard about what the screen can deliver well or badly.

said, a story holding very special meaning for you may urge truly imaginative solutions to its screen-translation problems.

No successful literary work ever translates easily to the screen. Each takes feats of co-creation from the film team, beginning most crucially with whoever adapts the story into a screenplay.

ASSIGNMENT

Research a Published Short Story for Adaptation as a Thirty-Minute Film

Try looking at anthologies from your own regional, cultural, or ethnic background. They may usefully reflect your interests and experiences. Read any material that strongly attracts you a second time, and decide how difficult it would be to translate by looking at the story purely as screen action. Much fiction exerts a powerful mood but on closer examination uses a special literary approach or style that has no ready screen equivalent. An author might, for instance, concentrate on the main character's consciousness and tell the story from an interior, subjective view. This is likely to present overwhelming difficulties for screen adaptation. Interior consciousness cannot be put on film except as a narration, which is usually clumsy and literary in feeling.

As we have said before, we can never enter another person's being in life. We have to infer that person's interior state from the evidence of their exterior actions, both physical and verbal. Likewise in mainstream cinema, the film audience observes and assesses from external *evidence*, rather than, as in literature, being privileged to share an author's or character's verbalization of consciousness. What I say here is a guide, not immutable law, since film history contains all sorts of radical experiments.

In film, literature, and all the other arts, the audience's relationship to the medium is a fascinating and complex issue. But here our object is to explore the fundamentals.

Report

In a portfolio, include a photocopy of the story and write:

1. Title, author, and a brief summary of its action.
2. Definition of the author's underlying meaning and purpose in writing this story.
3. Notes on problems and particular strengths in the piece, answering these questions:
   a. Who is the main character?
   b. Through whose point of view is the story seen? Would you want or need to change this?
   c. Discuss problems in adapting the story, such as:

- Are the main characters' inner lives sufficiently externalized through action? If not, how could this be improved?
- Are there enough characters, or too many? (In a single-character story, her internal decision to do something important might have to be verbalized to another character invented specially for the purpose. Then you'd have to build that character into the story in other ways, so he doesn't blatantly exist to solve a narrative problem).
- How are the necessary motivations and backgrounds for each of the characters conveyed?
- Is the main dilemma for the main character (or characters) strongly evidenced?
- Is the main character's development sufficient and interesting enough?
- Are there any remaining aspects to the adaptation that need comment?

EXAMPLES

Example 1: "An Encounter," from *Dubliners*, by James Joyce (Peter Riley)

Summary. The narrator of "An Encounter" is a young Irish boy bored with the monotony of school life and the Wild West games that he and his friends play in the evenings. Along with two classmates he decides to skip school and go on an adventure: a journey down to the port in Dublin, and a ferry crossing to a place called the "Pigeon House" near Ringsend. One of the boys, fearful of reprisals, does not turn up at the appointed time. But Mahony, a tough kid armed with a slingshot, meets the narrator and the two set off on their journey.

The boys enjoy themselves down at the wharf, watching the ships, eating lunch with the sailors. They cross the river in the ferry and wander through Ringsend, buying biscuits in the local shops and chasing a stray cat through the street. Eventually they realize they are too tired to continue their journey and rest in a field before turning back.

As the two sit there, a bizarre old man in a ratty green-black suit and odd hat passes them, then turns to come back their way. He sits down next to them and asks them about school and books, identifying the narrator as one who is a "bookworm" like himself, not one "for games" like Mahony. With a smile that reveals the gaps in his yellowed teeth, the man interrogates them about the many "sweethearts" they each must surely have. He continues, speaking about how much he admires beautiful young girls. The narrator is wary of this strange figure, who gets up as suddenly as he sat down and walks away.

But the man turns around again and returns to the boys' side. Mahony darts off after the cat they were chasing, and the old man remains silent next to the narrator. Then he breaks into a frightening monologue about whipping insolent young boys, how boys who have sweethearts and keep secrets should be whipped without mercy. He tells the narrator he would "whip such a boy as if he were unfolding some elaborate mystery."

The narrator, disturbed and afraid, leaps up and pretends to tie his shoe. Then he bids the man goodbye and climbs the slope of the field, fearful that the man will grab him by the ankles. He calls to Mahony across the field, and the other boy mercifully comes to his rescue.

The Author's Underlying Purpose. Joyce shows how those who would seek a world of adventure are confronted with the unsavory elements that such a world harbors. By flouting the conventional, rigid codes of home and school, the adventurer is faced with a terrifying truth. For the old man identifies the narrator as belonging more to his world than to the world he left behind. The narrator cannot simply close his eyes to "darker things."

Problems/Strengths. Because "An Encounter" is told entirely in the first person, some problems arise, particularly in the opening pages wherein the narrator describes activities and brief situations that span a great deal of time. But these passages could easily be altered for the purposes of a short film. The narrative voice is a strong one, and it might be interesting to use some narration, [perhaps] an older man looking back on a formative encounter of his youth. This piece relates quite closely to my themes in that it once again deals with individuals taking steps over boundaries and confronting something darker. The narrator's life can never be the same now that he knows what exists on the fringes of his safe world. He will not have the simple, blind life that Mahony is intended to lead.

Peter is right; that this story is told in the first person does poses problems. However, if we ask, "To whom might the main character be telling the story?" we find that he could be telling it later to friends in the school dormitory, or maybe years later to the boy who didn't show up, now an adult.

In the telling, his narrated memories could turn into present-tense happenings. This device threatens to be clumsy and artificial unless the listener can play some part that makes him an active participant and not just a narrative convenience. Even a great work like *Wuthering Heights* is flawed in this regard, because it uses a servant who plays no other part in the events. She exists simply to narrate the story. The reader quickly forgets her in a book, but she cannot be such a passive presence in a film. Seeing her present and doing nothing, we would question her function.

A strength in Peter's choice is that the action begins from the characters' rejecting the suffocating, sheltered world of their school in favor of the unknown delights of the docklands. In the heady new environment they become energetic and questing adventurers—until, that is, the advent of the perplexing older man, whose dominant characteristic is sexual frustration.

About him, we must a key question, one that can clarify the nature and purpose of any real-life or fictional character: *What is he/she trying to do or get?*

The older man might be hoping for a vicarious sexual experience by persuading the boy to share some amorous experience. However, the reader guesses that these boys have no relationship with girls and that the older man knows this. His affect suggests something more unsettling: pedophiliac motivations. From his flattering and chummy manner, it's plain he is skillfully probing the nature of the boy's sexual feelings to discover where he may be vulnerable. The sensitive, Joycean boy narrator, feeling the depraved heat of the man's homoerotic sexuality, senses treachery and flees. His friend Mahony is, however, untouched. His sensibilities are too coarse to have this receptiveness.

> *"What is this character trying to do or get?"* is a constant question to ask if one is to get inside any character. Answering it always yields new subtexts, new underlying motivations. From these you can assemble something of larger meaning. Practice this during the real-life interchanges going on around you. This simple little question uncovers an endless profusion of hidden agendas. For the ultimate challenge, include yourself among the characters you analyze.

What makes the story poignant is that, being young and sheltered, the boy may now feel that all adult sexuality is tainted.

Example 2, "Le Diner de Cons," by Francis Veber (Louis Leterrier)

This short story is fairly recent. Its French title can be translated as "Dumb Supper." The author is Francis Veber, a well-known French author-director. Some of his most famous work has been remade in such Hollywood films as *The Toy* or more recently *The Birdcage*.

Summary.   It's Thursday night and for Peter Brochant and his friends it is Dumb Supper day. The rule of this game is rather simple: Each brings along the most stupid person they could find. The person that has discovered the most spectacularly simpleminded is declared the winner.

Tonight, Peter is ecstatic: he has found a rare pearl of dumbness. The ideal retard. "A World class dummy!" Frankie Pigeon, public servant pee-on at the Internal Revenue Service. Frankie's only passions are the models he makes with matches.

But what Peter doesn't know is that Frankie more than anything else is one of the most unlucky people, and one of the masters in creating catastrophes. . . .

But tonight Peter doesn't feel that great because he's thrown out his back. He tries to call the meeting off. But he has no way of contacting Frankie on time, so Frankie will arrive at Peter's luxurious apartment and, alarmed by Peter's situation, will decide to stay with Peter and refuse all of his host's invitations to leave. This is the beginning of a long nightmare for Peter Brochant, in which his entire universe crumbles around him.

> In cinema as in life, *a development in someone's feelings is best evidenced by what he or she does.* Too often screenwriters rely on dialogue or facial expressions to convey important inner changes, but this is only another form of *narrating.* More effective evidence is a series of unfolding actions.

The Author's Underlying Purpose.   The author's underlying purpose is to show first that the richest and most intelligent people are most of the time not the happiest people alive. They have so many skeletons in their closet that it is sometimes hard to contain them all. Also the superiority complex they constantly carry is sometimes unbearable, especially when they realize that the people whom they consider inferior are most of the time better off being that way in this world. His purpose is therefore rather simple. It is a gentle criticism of today's society where, even if we believe that class divisions have vanished, they are still very much present.

Problems/Strengths.   Strange coincidences are pivotal in this story. Its compression—the entire action taking place in one evening and in one location (Peter Brochant's apartment)—is both the strength and weakness of this piece. Sometimes this becomes repetitive, and the other characters who interact in the rest of the piece with our two protagonists feel a little hemmed in. Another strength is because it is rather original, especially in America, to see this kind of story applied in that kind of setting. If we were to adapt this story for the screen, its cost would be ridiculously cheap. Isn't that all we are looking for when writing a short film?

At the end of the story Peter eventually realizes his mistake in misjudging his guest. He will find a new friend in Frankie and reevaluate all of his life in the process. This moral falls inside two of my themes: We find our most sincere friends in the strangest of places and situations, and the idea that several steps must be passed in order to develop one's own identity. There is a little bit of Peter Brochant in every one of us. No one is open-minded enough.

This story may also prove difficult to adapt for the screen. Here the development one anticipates for a main character is an inner one. It shows externally only as a gradual, incremental relaxation of Peter's judgments. Louis is understandably taken with the story's moral purpose—that our first valuations are usually based on nothing more than prejudice—but he doesn't say how the all-important steps in Peter's inner transformation are made outwardly visible. Any film about a change of heart depends for its success on being able to show a series of clear behavioral steps. Then its actors can portray each turning point.

Every screen narrative—whether comedy, tragedy, or anything else— depends on being realized as a series of behavioral sequences where each links to the next, like building-blocks. The art of adaptation lies in turning a literary work into a stream of sequences, each comprising behavioral and visual evidence for the audience to judge. The next stages of development in Louis's adaptation would be to block out these steps in his main character's development, and then to find behavioral clues that will hint at the changes Peter is experiencing—not easy.

Anticipation. Effective drama presents a story as a series of behavioral building-blocks. Each scene aims to pose puzzles and fill us with anticipation about the outcome, wanting to know "what will happen next." When characters must choose, we are drawn into assessing what they will do, and why. Intelligent drama delays resolving these situations as long as possible, so we exercise our imagination and judgment. The delay ensures that we are an active audience, not one that waits passively.

Example 3: "The Vigilante," by Victor Schiff (Chris Darner)

Summary. "The Vigilante" is a past-tense recollection of a single night, from the perspective of the main character. Although never directly identified by name or identity, beyond that he is the person who did what he did that night, the main character's personality is revealed through his thoughts and reactions to the events that unfold. It opens with details of a covert activity somewhere in Pennsylvania. As the story quickly progresses we learn that the night will include the tarring and feathering of a local unionizer. Although the setting is not the South, the participants decide to don [Ku Klux Klan] hood and cloak and make the event look racially motivated. Brief sketches of detail splash through the story and it climaxes with the victim indeed being tarred and feathered. The story ends with the main character explaining that the victim died as a result of the tarring, and admitting to himself that "... I can't sleep any more. I never killed a man before."

The Author's Underlying Purpose.   The style of the story is unique and is the primary reason I was drawn to it. Schiff weaves the details of the story very interestingly, mixing the backstory and events that led to the tarring with the present gruesome details of the event, in a moment-to-moment, as-it-happens realism. Then, at the end of the piece, through manipulating the main character's voice, the story is given a more "told" feeling, with the events all relating to the main character's current problem of living with himself after killing someone.

I think the style of the piece is intimately related to its subtext. A person just like the reader is brought to do the ugliest of things. Caught up in the moment and surrounded by a maelstrom of twisted support he temporarily escapes the confines of his better judgment and moral responsibility.

Problems/Strengths.   As happens with much prose, especially short stories, the interior nature of the piece would prove problematic in a piece for a cinema audience. Interestingly, by the end of the story the reader is sympathetic to the main character, even after reading he was part of something so ugly. This is achieved by slowly revealing that he is caught up in actions in which he would really rather not be involved. However, this sympathy is generated solely through his internal doubts and questions. If the story were

told only through external means such as actions and dialogue, a much different (and less sympathetic) portrait of
this character might be painted. The subtlety could easily be
lost when adapting the piece to the screen. Possible solutions might be voice-over and manipulation of the photo-
graphic image to portray a distorted and disturbing vision
of the present, mixed with a more natural portrayal of the
past. The film version could also end in a documentary-style
interview with the main character to give an honesty and
integrity to his conclusions looking back on the event.

While the various shooting styles may seem difficult to
fuse into one piece, I feel that this melding would make for
a very visually interesting film. Combining these elements
would, I feel, maintain the integrity and charm that Schiff's
story carries so well.

The weaving of different times, places and emotions on
the page seems particularly tricky to adapt to film, but I feel
by using the techniques I have outlined above, something
unique and interesting could be brought to the screen.

I think I was originally drawn to this piece because of the
challenge in adapting it to the screen. Looking at it thematically, however, I see that there is a theme at the heart of this
short story that ties strongly to my theme list: A man, a man
like any other, looking down at his hands and realizing that
he is looking at the hands of a killer.

Here is another highly complex, internalized piece that bristles with difficulties for screen adaptation. Chris is clear that the tarring and feathering is
being replayed obsessively inside the point-of-view character's mind, and
that the inwardly seen past is interwoven with an externally experienced
present. Though the events are fairly straightforward, the story focuses
on the main character's moral contemplation of them, and on the self-
indictment implied by his sleeplessness and recurring memories. While
others who are less principled or less sensitive to the suffering they inflicted
have moved on, this vigilante has not. He is that haunted figure, the moral
man who followed the crowd and suffers a terrible awakening. The story
paints a cross-section of his tortured consciousness, which doesn't or can't
lead him to take action or develop in some other way. This works well as a
short story because literature can easily deliver an inwardly experienced
stream of consciousness.

However, in a film about an isolated character, we can only infer what he
feels and thinks through his behavior. But the vigilante is condemned to
relive his supreme failure through memory rather than consciously by word
or deed. He is not articulate, introspective, or engaged in any action. We have
access to what he sees in his mind's eye, and this recreates his history for us,
but in a film unless he *does* something, we can only guess at how he feels

toward it. His inaction and lack of developing consciousness will be hard to justify, and we will wonder why he doesn't act in some new way. A documentary quality, or an interview, might admit rather too obviously that fictional techniques have failed to solve a narrative problem.

DISCUSSION

All three examples are told through the main characters' minds and perceptions. This is not surprising, since most successful short stories capitalize on what literature alone can do. This means that the best stories are especially challenging to a filmmaker. Paradoxically, second-rate literature is often more amenable to adaptation, because it is likely to be more melodramatic and thus cinematic. Jean-Luc Godard made no secret of taking some of his plot lines from pulp fiction. Conversely, when a great novel is stripped of its interior, contemplative qualities for a screen version and boiled down to its action line, it often becomes a travesty of the original.

To shop well for stories in literature takes a rather strong and confident vision of how one intends to use the screen. Until experience teaches this clarity, one is vulnerable to the seduction of words—though that is hardly the worst of fates. Possibly an inspiring story will bring inspiration as one tries to turn words into the more concrete tools of film narrative. Here (can you tell?) I speak ruefully, having failed myself.

Of course, these three stories might still become first-rate films, since the writers have only made a preliminary assessment. This stage is the first skirmish, with the serious battle waiting down the road. Never be deterred from a story you really, really like until you have done considerable work at laying bare, then solving, its particular problems. This brings its own fascination and enlightenment.

GOING FARTHER

More often than not, a short story can contain the kernel of a whole feature film, and the screen version may well surpass the original. Nicholas Roeg's mystery *Don't Look Now* (1971) is taken from a short story by Daphne du Maurier; it is a superb, tight, highly cinematic development of du Maurier's fascination with the mysteries beyond death. Sidney Pollack's *Out of Africa* (1985) was developed from a slender autobiographical tale by Isak Dinesen, supplemented by episodes from biographies about her. Hitchcock's *Rear Window* (1954) was adapted from Cornell Woolrich's "It Had to Be Murder"; like all his films, it takes on a life of its own.

Here are some studies of the adaptation process. The Skaggs volumes are invaluable supplements to films made from classic short-story origins. In case I sound too negative about subjective short stories, John Korty's masterly film *The Music School* (1976) is generated from a five-and-a-half-page story by John Updike entirely set in a man's mind.

Bluestone, George. *Novels into Film*. Berkeley, CA: University of California Press, 1957. (Another old book, also out of print, that does a good job of comparison. Assesses adaptations of such classics as *Wuthering Heights, Pride and Prejudice, The Grapes of Wrath,* and *Madame Bovary.*)

Richardson, Robert. *Literature and Film*. Bloomington: Indiana University Press, 1969. (Now out of print, this remains a lucid and intelligent comparison of fundamentals in the languages of literature and film.)

Seger, Linda. *The Art of Adaptation: Turning Fact and Fiction into Film*. New York: Henry Holt, 1992. (Down-to-earth exploration of literature, theatre, and real-life stories as origins for films, with a chapter on that two-headed beast, docudrama.)

Skaggs, Calvin. *The American Short Story*. New York: Dell, vol. 1 reissued 1997, vol. 2 reissued 1989. (This is a fabulous set. You get a superb collection of classic stories [Cather, Crane, Faulkner, Fitzgerald, Hawthorne, Hemingway, James, O'Connor, Thurber, Updike, Wright]. You also get the scripts that were made for the American Short Story film series, as well as a high-level critical essay on each story. If you can also, through interlibrary loan or an esoteric videotheque,[1] get hold of any of the films as well, you will have a whole schooling in adaptation at your disposal.)

1. Such as Facets Multimedia, which has thirty-three thousand classic titles for hire or sale. They can be reached at 1517 West Fullerton Avenue, Chicago, Illinois, 60614 (toll free 1-800-532-2387, fax 1-773-281-2206) or through their Website, http://www.facets.org. Note that their tapes are in NTSC only.

12

News Story

The goal in this chapter is to use a newspaper story as a resource. We are going to cast aside the rules of good journalism and, as an exercise in thematic expression, make a deliberately self-centered use of actuality.

Imagine that a wealthy eccentric offers you a ten-minute slot on national television. You can fill it with any short, factually based movie of your own making. Further, you are told that the conventional restraints of objectivity and political balance are unimportant, that you must instead use real events to express covertly your private concerns and values.

Of course, indoctrination emerges from the media all the time, but for expediency it is skillfully masked. Fascinating though the ethics of this are, we won't pause to debate the rights or wrongs here. Instead, as an exercise in mining ideas from the real world, go ahead and proselytize. This need not lead to utterly one-sided propaganda, since the full range of drama is continually reappearing in everyday life. See if you can suggest the complexity of life yet employ real events as a way to air your closest concerns and transmit your own values.

Propaganda and drama are different. Drama draws us into the dilemmas of people contending with complex and often contradictory forces. It shows options and lets us draw our own conclusions. Propaganda, on the contrary, employs any means necessary to persuade us to accept an agenda of dogma and foregone conclusions.

ASSIGNMENT

Choice of Material

Pick a news story and make it serve as a television vehicle for your own thematic interests. From newspapers or magazines, find a short and appealing piece that is little known and could make a ten-minute actuality item for television. Try to choose a news story, preferably unusual, that holds a strong underlying meaning for yourself and thus, potentially, for your audience. Write:

1. A summary of the news item's factual content.
2. How it might best be covered and presented. Avoid the usual paraphernalia of presenters, reporters, experts, and talking-head interviews. The aim is to put the audience in direct contact with the characters and eliminate the conventional intermediaries. What you can use is:

     Archive footage, if it could reasonably exist.

     Any action that could still be filmed after the event.

     Recorded sound interviews that can be used as "interior monologues" for a main character or characters. These have been evoked by an interviewer, but the interviewer's questions have been eliminated.
3. Comment on your purpose for choosing the story.
4. Comment on the news item's strengths and weaknesses.

Analysis

Write notes defining the underlying meaning and significance of the event. Since you are making actuality serve your own didactic ends, pick a form for your story that best serves what you want to get across.

EXAMPLES

Example 1: *Villagers Climb Popocatepetl, Leave Offerings* (Angela Galyean)

Summary.   Early March, 1996 a handful of locals of Xalitz-intla, Mexico, climbed the Popocatepetl volcano to bring strange, but religious, offerings of fruit and spicy mole sauce. They climbed up in an attempt to appease the patron saint of the volcano, San Gregorio Chino. In a combined ritual of Roman Catholic and Indian tradition, the people of Xalitzintla placed fruit and chocolate-based chili in the mouth of the recently reactivated volcano.

The day before the offering was made, the volcano had emitted steam and ash for the first time since 1664. Of Aztec origin, the name Popocatepetl means "smoking mountain" and that is precisely what it did. Engraved across the horizon was a steady plume of smoke that snaked its way across the Mexican sky. Television footage showed two sep-

arate emissions—one from the crater and another from a
fissure to the east.

The villagers are living in a constant state of paranoia and
alarm. They are praying that evacuation will not be necessary and they will continue to bring offerings in hopes that
this will calm the saint.

Purpose.   From this story, I got a clear picture of a culture's
community spirit and union against nature. Turning to religion or spirituality in crisis is almost outdated, at least in
American society. I found this story refreshing in its
undying faith and organic purity.

Problems/Strengths.   I would like to present an objective
portrait of these people and their efforts. In ten minutes of
film, an entire community's philosophy could easily be com-
municated in simple documentation of village life and the
specific philosophy of the religious events. Short interviews,
moving landscapes, and footage of the ceremonies could
create a simple, precious, and inspirational story.

This event embraces the antithesis of one of my mar-
ginally pessimistic themes—"good guys finish last." The
theme of this piece (providing the outcome is positive)
promotes faith and respect for the supernatural. Religion,
having a "good guys" association, enforces the importance
of being good and inspiring this within your community.
The upbeat message would be that good guys don't always
finish last.

The faith and rugged courage of the Mexican peasants attracts this author
as a refreshing antidote to the cynical and materialistic civilization into
which she was born. Until she chose this story and thought over why she
had picked it, she was unaware of how much optimism she carried inside
her. So the assignment served as a catalyst. Contrary to her own fears about
goodness generally going unrewarded, she finds that she gravitates toward
its very opposite—a real-life event where villagers pit the faith of their ances-
tors against Nature's most primordial forces.

To Nature, city dwellers ascribe all that is green, natural, and good, but
to peasants living on the brink of subsistence she is cruelly changeable and
her forces casually conspire to ruin them and drive them into starvation.
Toward such powers, these Mexican Indians turn a face of humility and pro-
pitiation, pledging to the gods in order to stave off destruction. It is impres-
sive that they take responsibility for the imbalance of forces in their world
rather than fatalistically shrugging their shoulders and putting the blame
elsewhere.

Reacting this way may be risky when dealing with volcanoes, but under other circumstances it is enlightened to take responsibility and attempt to harmonize with the forces around you. In the documentary *La Soufriére* (Werner Herzog, Germany, 1976), the director and his crew go to an island where a volcano threatens to explode. While exploring their own (scared newsreel photographers') relationship with the impending cataclysm, they come across an impoverished mountainside farmer. He has decided not to leave his farm and rests peacefully among his beloved animals. Serenely he leaves his fate in God's hands. What will be, will be! His tranquillity, unlike our turmoil as we imagine fate moving beyond our control, is salutary, and Herzog makes us take full notice.

Example 2: *Inmates Find Personal Freedom in Dance Program* (Amanda McCormick)

Summary.   The article details how a dance program at a women's prison in Washington State helps the inmates vent frustration and express vulnerability in constructive, creative ways. It presents a night of performance from the dancers, who cull material from personal journal entries. Many of the performers have never had a venue in which to discuss or express their feelings toward their lives, their crimes, or the experience of being incarcerated. The article details individual participants and the ways that the dance program has shaped their lives.

Purpose.   This story is significant for its contrasts. It has a prison setting, where the inmates are, needless to say, deprived of much freedom of movement. The dance improv and journal exercises not only give the women a voice, but also some "room to move." So the dance program helps to adjust the mental imprisonment that may have been a part of the women's lives even *before* they found themselves behind bars. *Personal* freedom, and the freedom to express what they feel, may be the freedoms they lack most, beyond their physical imprisonment.

Problems/Strengths.   In this situation, it would be fascinating to track these women and see how participating in the dance program may have affected their lives. Barring that possibility, this sort of story lends itself to hearing the voices of individual participants in interview, and perhaps, recording the conception and development of a dance piece. It would be interesting to explore how the women translate their experience into movement and non-verbal expression.

I don't immediately see a connection to the themes that I
turned in for this class, but the story appeals to me
immensely on some level. I am interested in the way that
dance is an expression of the most visceral emotion, but in
this instance it can become more than cathartic; for these
women it is potentially an opportunity for growth, a way of
liberating themselves from their imprisonment. I find that
kind of empowerment fascinating, and for that reason think
it is a rich story source.

The writer's idea is to show in ten minutes the evolution of the dance-
making process and also its ability to express something ineffable that
emerges through movement rather than words. She is drawn to this subject
because it enacts a cherished belief—that dance developed from recollection
encourages the expression of deep-rooted emotion. She believes that express-
ing what has happened in your life, and how you feel about it, can make
you free—even in a prison.

Applying this idea to people in jail implies that we are in bondage until
we tell (or better, perform) our story to an audience. I must say I agree.
Everyone has a story, and a vital part of freeing oneself lies in getting one's
view of it heard and accepted—preferably by a group.

Example 3: *News Story* (Yoo Kyung Park)

Summary.   The most powerful and popular [Korean] pop
group suddenly decided to retire. The group had three
members: One whose name is Taji mainly writes all of their
songs and lyrics. Others, whose names are Hyun-Suk and
Juno, make new dances.
They were unique be-
cause most of the other
Korean pop singers sing
about love between a man
and a woman. This group
sings about social prob-
lems, North and South
Korea's reunification, and
serious educational prob-
lems, etc. And they mixed
Korean traditional music
with Western rap music.

They started their
career like other musi-
cians. The style of their
first album is exactly the

*The camera and microphone can only
reproduce the specific.* Unlike
literature, they cannot handle
generalities or abstractions. The
beliefs, moods, or ideas you want to
show must reach the audience
through an artfully constructed
accumulation of credible action. You
can of course make your characters
debate them, but this usually looks
artificial. These problems exist
because *film, like human consciousness,
is always in the present.* It cannot
move to the past tense like literature
and stay there. For every flashback
quickly becomes a new present.

same as [the type of] American pop song which is the most popular genre. But once they were successful, they started to differentiate themselves. They became more unique as they were also doing their own music style. Some people were more crazy about them, but some didn't like them. Especially, the Korean censorship system was against them whenever they made a new album because many of their songs criticized problems of Korean society and the hypocrisy of adults. After they made five albums, they suddenly disappeared and said that they would not be doing music any more. People don't know exactly why they decided to retire, but there is much gossip about it. And one story is about the pressure of some powerful group.

Underlying Meaning. A young challenging spirit is crushed by some powerful group. Things that should be covered: Their will and hard work to make great songs which have messages for young people and that conflicts with existing power groups. A young challenging spirit seems crushed by an existing power group such as the censorship system and the mass media. But even though the group decided not to do music any more, their songs will affect many young people.

I am fascinated by the issues that preoccupy writers from other cultures. Young Koreans I have taught often seem to focus on how fear is used to control people, on pressures to conform or on the authoritarian use of power. These are abstract issues that are easier to handle in nonfiction cinema, because there they can be discussed (see sidebar). Yoo Kyung believes that whoever sings truthfully cannot be suppressed. Undoubtedly it will be the brave (who are usually the young) who will press toward change, as we have seen so often. It is their songwriters, poets, playwrights, and movie makers who coalesce the public's thoughts and feelings and prepare it for some kind of action.

Unless she can strongly imply what pressures, sinister or otherwise, caused the group to disband, this would be a difficult film to make, because the group has already gone silent. Her story lies in the uneasy space between the moment that the group decided to disband and the symptoms that evidence how their music is changing hearts and minds.

Summary

What is interesting about all three news story adaptations is that each does indeed arise from a belief held by the writer. Of course the assignment encourages this to happen, but as in fictional assignments, convictions invariably emerge when the writer is emotionally engaged. Let's look at a method to ensure that topic and belief are united whenever you set out to create a story.

MAKING A WORKING HYPOTHESIS

Making your beliefs and intentions into a *working hypothesis* is tremendously useful when you are developing either fiction or nonfiction work. To do this, just complete the following sentences.

In life I believe that. . . . (your belief)
I will show this in action through (topic). . . .
The main conflict is between . . . and. . . .
The point of view character(s) will be. . . .
I want my audience to realize that. . . .
And to feel that. . . .

Had the writers made up a working hypothesis statement for their news story writings, they might look like this:

	"Villagers Climb Popocatepetl."	"Inmates Find Personal Freedom in Dance Program."	"Disbanding the Band."
1. **In life I believe that. . . .**	people find peace and dignity when they seek harmony with ineluctable forces.	freedom of the spirit is more important than freedom of the body.	truth liberates.
2. **I will show this in action through. . . .**	showing poor Mexicans of faith propitiating the forces of nature that threaten their village.	following prison inmates developing a dance from their journal entries.	following the development of a protest event that plans to use the band's music and lyrics.
3. **The main conflict is between. . . .**	the frightful power of the brooding volcano and the steady, fearless faith of the believers.	the need to tell one's story and the fear of exposing oneself.	the demonstrators's need to be public and the police intentions to arrest them.
4. **The main point of view character will be. . . .**	the village shaman.	one inmate making one dance.	a secret police informer who sees the demonstrators and their music as unpatriotic.

	"Villagers Climb Popocatepetl."	"Inmates Find Personal Freedom in Dance Program."	"Disbanding the Band."
5. **I want my audience to realize that. . . .**	faith and acceptance are useful qualities throughout life.	a wordless physical process like mime or dance can well represent a woman's relationship with her own past.	no amount of repression can undo truth once it is out in the open.
6. **And to feel that. . . .**	Mexican villagers can teach us by example how to relate to forces outside our control.	the activity of creating her autobiography is spiritually liberating.	these young people will probably be beaten—for now.

The working hypothesis is a powerful tool for organizing your initial ideas into a flow of narrative intentions. That flow is the vehicle by which you project your ideas and abstract intentions into your audience.

In planning news coverage or a documentary, one usually shoots with no sure knowledge of the outcome, so any ideas that contribute a storytelling form are especially useful. As my colleague Chap Freeman once pointed out, the working hypothesis builds a bridge between personal belief at the beginning and the hearts and minds of the audience at the end.

> Make a *working hypothesis* for either documentary or fiction. It forces you to define what your piece is really about and to specify how you intend to evoke ideas and feelings in your audience. Make one after the first draft. Redraft it as often as you incorporate large changes. Use the process as a reality check and to see your ideas grow.

A working hypothesis therefore defines a *dramatic delivery system*, one that you constantly amend as research, new experience, and better ideas follow on.

Though the working hypothesis idea was designed for documentary, it works equally well for fiction. Using it causes you to define thoroughly what you are trying to accomplish. Strangely enough, many working for the screen, particularly fiction writers, never articulate this. When challenged they find that they cannot describe their goals. Needless to say, knowing where you are going makes for a better journey and a surer arrival.

Countless fiction pieces start from newspaper stories. Some are subtitled "From a True Story," but many more are not. There are solid reasons to start from actuality and then obscure its origins. You know what it is in the story that attracts you, and you want to find out more by working it through in writing. (See the dedication to this book: "Nothing is real until I have written about it.") Because it happened in real life, you know that you are dealing with something inherently credible. By blurring its origins you give yourself the freedom to ascribe actions and motives that will provide a greater sense of insight than afforded by the original. Essentially this is using drama as a tool to probe reality. Its equivalent in documentary, "docudrama," is an ethically slippery and hard-to-use form that many people nevertheless find fascinating.

GOING FARTHER

Here are some sources for those interested in, working creatively with non-fiction, deriving story ideas from actuality, and melding documentary and fiction together.

Hemley, Robin. *Turning Life into Fiction.* Cincinnati, OH: Story Press, 1994. (Transforming real life into stories, gaining psychic distance between memoir and fiction, and the ethical and self-protective considerations that arise when you take liberties with fact.)

Rabiger, Michael. *Directing the Documentary*, 3d ed. Boston: Focal Press, 1998. (For a brief overview of the way documentary has been used over its decades of existence, see chapter 2, "A Brief and Functional History of the Documentary." Chapters 3 and 4 deal with finding and developing documentary ideas, and chapters 8 and 9 deal with research and developing a proposal, including the working hypothesis.)

Rosenthal, Alan. *Why Docudrama? Fact-Fiction on Film and TV.* Carbondale, IL: Southern Illinois Press, 1999. (An excellent anthology of essays laying out the history, principles, and uses of this sometimes treacherously hybrid form.)

Seger, Linda. *The Art of Adaptation: Turning Fact and Fiction into Film.* New York: Henry Holt, 1992. (Down-to-earth exploration of literature, theater, and real-life stories as origins for films, and a chapter on docudrama.)

13

A Documentary Subject

Making documentary is fascinating, because it confirms how often ordinary people live richly dramatic lives. But no story exists ready made. If you want to portray a San Francisco ascetic, a mine-clearing squad, or a young bride somewhere in Africa, the challenge is always the same: to figure out what story to tell, and what point of view to take within any given situation. Like an artist deciding what sculpture lies within the block of stone, the documentary maker must decide what story and meaning await liberation from the plethora of actuality that obscures every subject.

Modern documentary seldom arranges life for the camera; it prefers to capture life as it happens. Since life is often unpredictable, the documentarian gambles on getting a combination of what can reasonably be anticipated as gifts (or blows) from the gods. Randomness may not be a problem. For example, if you are going to film a group of enthusiasts reenacting a Civil War battle, you can discover the shape of events in advance, when and where things will happen, simply because there is a plan, and your warriors keep to it. If, however, you set out to cover a volatile marital situation, every event may have several possible outcomes and produce any amount of the unexpected. For each situation you would need different shooting strategies.

> *Direct cinema* and *cinéma vérité* are different philosophies of making documentary. Direct cinema uses an observational camera, tries not to intercede or disturb its subject, and hopes to catch interesting truths as they happen. *Cinéma vérité* sees intercession by, or interaction with, the makers as a valid part of filmmaking. It allows the filmmakers to catalyze responses or events, which in turn reveal underlying truths.

Making documentary appeals to those who like to enter new situations and improvise accounts as life unfolds. For the purpose of this chapter's assignment, however, we will keep it simple and concentrate on stories that have already happened or that have a predictable body of events. The goals are to:

- Find a real situation or event that interests you because it resonates to your chosen themes.
- Turn that situation into a factually based screen story that will serve your authorial purposes and interests.

Researching real people and real situations is highly productive, even for fiction afficionados with no intention of ever making a documentary. Novelists and screen-writers commonly undertake pain-staking research and spend much time immersing themselves in the kinds of people and situations they want to put in their work. No amount of imagination can ever rival the profundity and sheer oddity of the real.

> *Research.* Fiction writers give their work authority and depth by studying how real people handle real situations.

ASSIGNMENT

Choice of Subject

To develop a subject for your documentary film, choose from your news-clippings collection a situation that:

- Could be made into a film.
- Has inbuilt development in an event or character so the film won't merely unfurl some static, unchanging situation.
- Would engage your audience in some aspect of the real world. (To engross your audience means to involve it in ways that might be fascinating, disturbing, aggravating, frightening, funny, highly curious—you name it).

Your topic should involve us emotionally and provoke us into thinking critically about the important issues. Because interview-based films are too much like TV talk shows, documentary makers try to avoid them unless the interviewee is divulging matters that are unusual or deeply felt. Documentaries try to tell their stories using imagery, action, and behavior rather than narrating them through interviews. However, every rule has its exceptions. Apart from its famous reen-actment scenes, Errol Morris's *The Thin Blue Line* (1988) is nearly all "talking heads." But the characters, their story, and the presentation

> *Actions speak louder than words.* What people do is a better guide to their deepest feelings and intentions than anything they might say.

that Morris uses are so original and special that the film occupies a class all its own.

At the outset your film will need to establish some expository information as essential context. For instance, in a film about a failing farm you will need to show not only the victimization of the elderly farming couple but something (a loan manager scene, for instance) that sketches in the market forces that put such pressure on farmers. Let's say they mechanize so they can work larger and larger tracts of land. Why would they do that? Because supermarket chains have forced down the price of produce. Your job is to stimulate questions in the audience's minds, and provide enough answers to sustain the audience's interest.

> *Exposition* is the framework of facts and backstory that the audience needs to understand the characters and their issues. Exposition is least intrusive when concealed within the story's developing action.

Most human problems arise when vulnerable characters fall prey to a combination of inner and outer forces. You usually don't need to depict all of them—catalogs are the job of the social historian or sociologist—but the audience knows instinctively when a situation is fundamentally incomplete, unrealistically simplified, or rendered into the ideological monochrome of good versus evil. If, however, your farm going bust is shown through the perceptions of someone to whom the breakdown *is* a matter of good and evil (the teenage son, for instance), then you could make us feel the poignancy of his simplification, while sketching in the more complex forces that he is unable to appreciate.

> *Drama exists to investigate the complexity of the human condition.* Documentary is a branch of drama, and it should do more than present facts or reflect what would be visible to anybody present. It should select and confront us with human enigmas and puzzles to resolve. To illustrate solutions or preach what is right and wrong is the job of propaganda, not drama.

Like the best fiction films, documentaries are usually strongest when they show characters in action. Action is always in the present, while interviews often reflect events already resolved and now alive only in memory. Oral history can only be made in this way, but other subjects benefit greatly from being shot while they unfold. To watch two people inexpertly pilot a canoe down a fast river is far more gripping than hearing about it later. An observational camera shows their lack of skills and how danger is ever present. This is drama.

> *Dramatic tension* is the uncertainty the dramatist deliberately maintains to keep the audience involved and aware. Drama aims to confront us with evidence and make us use our critical and analytical faculties. This is why the courtroom is inherently dramatic.

Plan to film *evidence* that will make the audience see, feel, and think about the issues. Doing this well means deliberately orchestrating the conflict of different and opposing aspects. Though you want to show (not tell) what would lead a reasonable person toward your own conclusions, you want the outcome to remain uncertain for as long as possible, or you will look like a propagandist tiresomely expounding a cause.

> *We help to create our fate,* by making the choices dictated by our experience and temperament ("Character is fate"). When you create characters, or contemplate them in real life, ask yourself:
>
> - What is this person trying to get or do—in the short term and long term?
> - In each instance, what is stopping him or her?
> - How does he or she adapt to this?

Your paper should:

1. Give a brief outline of the background or context to the subject.
2. Say who your main character or characters is (are), and what the main predicament is. Let your film bring a magnifying glass to a situation that is small but significant. Resist the novice storyteller's urge to include everything life has taught you.
3. Explain what your film's underlying story organization would be. This usually means:
   - Considering how you will handle the progression of time in the movie.
   - Deciding whether the main character is the POV character or if there is another valid POV.
4. Describe any shooting, directing, interviewing, or juxtapositional editing techniques you think would be necessary to get the major points of your thematic argument across to your audience.

Analysis

Define:

1. The central conflict for the main character or characters. Think about this carefully, because few people go into this deeply enough.
2. The development in the main character (or characters) that you would hope to show.

EXAMPLES

Writing for a yet-to-be-shot documentary is perplexingly speculative. How, people ask, can one write about something that has not yet happened? In fact, one can and must. Too much theoretical preparation here would clog your mind; too little would leave you to stumble into a net of imponderables. In my NYU class I gave much less preparation, and in consequence the examples that follow reflect more what television shows as documentary than what the documentary form can be.

Example 1: Documentary Subject (Angela Galyean)

Timmy B——, ten years old, hated going to school. His truancy became so chronic that his parents took him to a psychiatrist who prescribed Prozac as treatment for Timmy's obstinacy. At first, Timmy's reaction to the drug was positive. It was not until the psychiatrist increased his dosage that Timmy began to experience violent mood swings. "He'd get really angry and stuff like that. He'd scream at you and then a few minutes later, he'd love you and hug you and not even remember being so angry," his mother, Cindy, said after the court hearing.

Only weeks after the start of Timmy's Prozac regimen, the fourth-grader grabbed his three-year-old niece as a human shield, aimed a twelve-gauge shotgun at a sheriff's deputy, and exclaimed, "I'd rather shoot you than go to school." It comes as no surprise that Timmy's lawyer blames this out- burst on the antidepressant drug.

Timmy's court case is the first known to involve a child using Prozac, which has not been proved [safe] for use in children for any condition. The drug's label notes that Prozac's safety and effectiveness for children has not been established. But Prozac is used to treat 56 percent of depressed children's cases because it has been proven effective for adults.

"Timmy B—— was under the influence of a mind-alter- ing drug at the time of the incident," the B——s' attorney noted. Prozac is the world's largest-selling antidepressant, with sales more than $1 billion a year. However, the drug's success has been clouded by claims that it causes violent mood swings and suicidal thoughts.

This story is particularly fascinating to me because it involves an obvious dysfunctional family situation and the mystery/fascination of today's Prozac. I have always feared the use of Prozac and have intimately experienced its effects on people I have known before, after, and during the use of the drug. This case is unusually interesting to me because it incorporates a child's life and mind. Timmy's life has been permanently damaged by a decision he did not make.

The film would first focus on Timmy, his parents, and the events of Timmy's life before he hated school, and therefore prior to seeing his psychiatrist. Then it would cover his experience in therapy, and the event itself. I would like to push ahead to examine what effects the trial is having on Timmy and what his life is like now that things have calmed down. I am only concerned with the cellular life of Timmy and the B——s, and this would make up the heart of the film.

By showing as much as I could of the lifestyle they had and have, I could translate a truly human experience made unique by Timmy. The narrative organization would depend on what response I got from the B——s, their community, and the participants of the court case. These people would be featured in the film, but my goal would be to show as little of the outside world as I could to parallel the entrapment of Timmy's mind while under the influence of the drug.

I have never made a documentary proper, so I would need to do miles of leg-work before diving into this project. It seems to me that this story might be able to tell itself, but I have a feeling that this is a common delusion of people making documentary films. Interviewing would need to be very intimate. Ideally, I would like to spend as much time as possible with the B——s so as to achieve ultimate comfort and ease within the interviews.

My particular moral stance on the subject of antidepressant drugs is quite simple. I think they are dangerous and unnecessary. That would have to be the moral slant the film would take, because I am very adamant and passionate about this subject. Going with the grain of the story, as I understand it, would be demonstrating a positive message in the minds of the participants, leading me to [hope for] further cooperation from the family. I tend to despise negative exposure in documentary subject films and plan to avoid that style at all costs.

Angela never spoke truer words than when she said, "This story might be able to tell itself, but I have a feeling that this is a common delusion of people making documentary films." Nevertheless, her strategy is quite practical, involving as it does dividing the film into three parts. These actually mirror the classic three-act drama (see sidebar and Figure 13–1).

1. *Backstory and exposition:* that is, life before using the drug, the boy's developing school phobia that led to his need for therapy.
2. *The struggle with a larger issue emerges.* A minor problem now turns into one much worse as he begins taking the drug. His problem changes from school phobia to wildly fluctuating mood swings and violence. This *inciting moment* develops to a crescendo in the

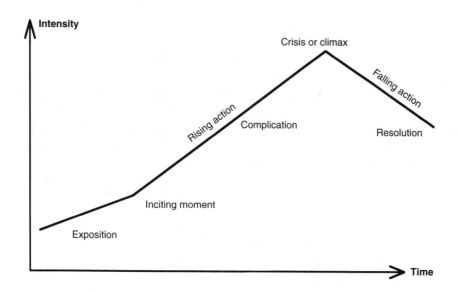

Figure 13–1   The Dramatic Curve: This is a way to plot the main events either in a scene or a whole story composed of many scenes. The coordinates are intensity (vertical) and the story's time line (horizontal). In conventional Western drama, Act I finishes before the inciting moment. Act II includes the inciting moment, complication (or *rising action*), and climax. Act III comprises the resolution, or *falling action*.

hostage-taking situation and, after his arrest, culminates in the rigmarole of a court case. The court decision probably represents the *climax* of the whole story.

3. *The resolution.* This is the only present-day section. It shows the aftereffects on the boy's daily life of the negative publicity and notoriety, and it questions whether the drug should be given at all, let alone to children.

Here we have a main character who is so out of kilter that he may remain unaware that he even has a problem, until Act III.

The classic *three-act structure* divides stage or screen drama into three dramatic blocks of unequal length. Their proportions are given as approximate percentages.

Act I (setup) develops the main character and the main problem or situation that he or she faces (25 percent).

Act II (confrontation) develops: the *inciting moment,* where the hero or heroine becomes committed to the struggle and the rising action begins; escalating *complications* and an intensifying struggle against hostile forces for a solution; and the *climax* (50 percent).

Act III (resolution) shows the *outcome* of the struggle (25 percent).

Interestingly, this structure is often also found within the individual scenes that contribute to the plot curve of the overall drama.

Where is the conflict that will make this piece dramatic? We might locate it in the awareness of the doctor who made the risky decision to use an undertested drug on a child, or in the parents who discovered too late that they had been overtrustful of the experts. Either way, the implications are far reaching and transcend Timmy's individual case. Consider:

- How desperate do a patient and his family have to become before a doctor should resort to less conservative treatment? Think of AIDS patients waiting in anguish while the Food and Drug Administration toils in slow motion through its testing procedures.
- What makes us trust experts, and when should we not? In the infamous Tuskegee experiments, poor southern black farmers were studied by the U.S. Public Health Service for forty years without ever being treated or told that they had syphilis. For sheer cruelty this rivals the Nazi medical experiments, and it is said to be a reason why African-Americans are apt to delay going to a doctor for treatment.

Angela's convictions lend authority to this film, because she carries scars from her own negative observation and thus starts from a clear position. I would recommend, were she actually making the film, that she avoid falling into partisan simplification, by contacting people who had been helped rather than hurt by the drug. Every drug has side-effects and (like all human beings and the ambiguity of their motives) can be a blessing or a curse depending on the user and the circumstances.

Example 2: Documentary Subject (Cynthia Merwarth)

The subject is teen suicide. The thought is to focus on three areas: The families and close friends that survive, who will discuss their feelings on the healing process and the possible signs they may have missed. A group of high school teens speak of the pressures they feel which push some of them to the edge. And then I would like to speak with a teen who has recently tried to commit suicide. It would be ideal to find out what the impact of their actions were upon themselves.

Teenage suicide is a problem that has mystified society. In this past decade, [mental health] practitioners have looked more seriously at the possible reasons that propel a teen into such a corner—for it is imperative to find out why death is seen as the only way out.

Suicide is one of the most private actions with public ramifications that a person can perform. It is a statement of their despair, a cry for help that was never heard. The consequence of such an act has profound outcomes on the people around the individual, including friends, family and even peers. Suicide is an invisible war and we are losing.

Making a film of this subject is important because it can hold out the possibility of hope in what is otherwise a hopeless situation. Through survivors we have the capacity to learn how to detect and act on potential suicide victims. We can learn how to help families deal with and talk about "taboo" issues, and come to a place of healing. We must, as a society, become more aware of a problem that too often robs great people of fulfilling their lives' natural paths.

This film will be [divided] into segments. I see it as a layered piece, focusing on one particular area at a time, then moving into other avenues of help and understanding. Breaking the documentary up will give the viewers more of a focus and help them to really understand what can be done to help themselves or someone they know. The focus will be on one facility worker, a family and a survivor—all the time looking into the more human side of healing. If one person is affected by this film it will be a success.

I plan on following a script, since the suggestions of visuals and commentary is more defined and the path more clear. The script will be more of a guideline, rather than something etched in stone. If I were to go the route of "cinéma vérité" I might run myself into an entirely different piece of work. Basically, I want as much pre-determined structure as I can get. This will be decided when I have the appropriate people chosen to represent a viewpoint. I would like unexpected events to become a positive attribute rather than something I must work around in the editing room.

Through juxtaposing direct images (a hotline worker; a group of teens; a potential suicide victim) I will reveal a world filled with misconceptions, and a lack of understanding toward the suicide victim and the people whom they affect. I will show the individual as they are, not as they believe they should be. That way I hope to attain candid conversations that reveal the simplicity and steadfastness of a decision having such decisive consequences.

The underlying theme that would run through the film is the effect a person's suicide has on those left behind after this terrible ordeal. It may not be appropriate to make a documentary based on teen suicide in the traditional interview format. The target audience for this program would be teenagers from the age of 13 to 18 and young adults to age 25. The intended audience is likely to contain adolescent suicide victims, so it's crucial to grab their attention on a subject they may not want to face. An alternative to the interview, [such as] the docu-drama format intertwined with real interviews, could work. This would show the story through dramatization: its characters, locations, and events. Through dialogue and action the viewer can understand behaviorally what the subject is going through. They may empathize better through entertainment than rhetoric, and understand that they are not alone.

The focus does not have to be on one particular individual, rather it may be on a group of young adults from different backgrounds and different geographic locations—all going through this secret battle with the self.

Unfortunately, I know too well how a person can be affected by a young adult's suicide for I am a survivor of this terrible social problem. Two young men I grew up with were victims, and a third just recently survived. They all knew one another, and the first boy who died I had known since the fourth grade. I was eighteen and unfortunately dealt with his death on my own (even though I had sought help from my university). Support groups for survivors were few in 1982. Friends cannot always talk to one another of such painful things and it is because of this that I am doing this film.

So passionate was Cynthia about this subject that she wrote far more than requested. For brevity I have edited her original. Like Angela, her stake in making this film is so clear that it easily dictates what path she wants to take. Through the power of the screen she wants us to know what it feels like to be young and suicidal, and to see the consequences of suicide on that person's family and friends. She wants nobody else to endure what she went through, and nobody else to cause it.

One might think that the main conflict for the suicidal person is being alone and that this is resolved by the act of killing oneself. Actually, Cynthia's proposal contains a series of consequences, rather than a depiction of the roots of conflict and possible resolutions. Conflict leads to choice between two or more actions, so choosing in itself isn't a conflict but the *result* of conflict. Hamlet's famous "To be, or not to be" soliloquy debates whether to confront all his troubles and revenge his father's death, or to commit suicide and follow him to

> *A character's conflict* is often wrongly assigned to his situation or feelings. Locate his conflict by looking at the nature of his or her main struggle. Ask, "Above all, what is this character trying to get or do, and what stops him?" What he is pushing against and what forces stop him form the nexus of a character's overarching conflict. In his daily pursuits there will be many minor conflicts, but they will all relate to the major one, if you have correctly identified it.

the grave. Those are his options, but his conflict arises from doubting that he has the courage and energy to see justice done on behalf of his murdered father.

It is difficult to think of suicide as representing a central character's development, since suicide terminates rather than resolves a problem. I think that development in Cynthia's film could probably come only from someone who had attempted suicide and thereafter came to understand other ways of dealing with their situation. Development might exist in friends and family who are arriving at a better understanding of the suicidal person's diminishing world and can now help someone else in danger. That requires the POV character(s) to be not the potential suicide but family and friends.

Another source of development might lie in placing an individual's suicidal despair in the larger context of young people searching for an acceptable identity. The person who died would then, perhaps, leave as his legacy a greater audience awareness of young people's search and vulnerability. It is interesting to consider that in war, when everyone has a heightened sense of having to fight to live, rates for both crime and suicide tend to plummet. This alone argues for looking at suicide differently.

Cynthia's plan to use a semidramatized form could help dispel the appearance of distance and objectivity that bedevils the traditional documentary. She wants to involve us closely in people's lives and actions, and to use reenactment to bring us closer. There is always, of course, the risk that life will eclipse art—that the actors will look embarrassingly inauthentic. The inverse risk is that the actors may be as credible as the "real" people, creating an ultimate confusion about who or what is "real" and thus authentic.

Example 3: "Hers: Pursuit of Happiness" (Michelle Arnove)

Two women, old friends from a distant country, live very similar lives in America. Both are married career women who have children, and they seem on the exterior to be liberated and Americanized. However, an underlying current emerges through a series of telephone conversations and both realize how different they really are from one another. Originating from Nigeria, Dympna and Nira within their homes have retained the customs and family traditions of the Ibo people, but present themselves as challenged and aggressive women in the world outside, that is, among American sensibilities. In the traditional Ibo culture, a woman is born, sometimes educated, marries, mothers children (preferably male) and yet accepts that her life must be lived through those of her husband and children. Hence, her personal identity is of little value, even if she lives her life in America and has a successful career. These are givens and are not challenged—and this works fine for both men and women when each knows their roles within the family unit. All is well.

However, one night Dympna receives a phone call from Nira confiding rather matter-of-factly that she is unhappy and is leaving her husband. While both women have shared intimate moments in their lives—weddings, childbirth, and the traditional rituals of the Ibo culture—there is something that sets them apart this evening. It is not until a few days later that Nira attempts to explain to her friend the internal changes that she is experiencing, and the decision she has made. She is prepared to face the consequences of her decision, one that would normally keep an Ibo woman from leaving her family to find her own happiness.

Regardless of American law, an Ibo woman who deserts her husband must leave as she supposedly came . . . with no money, no children, no support . . . nothing. In addition, she must pay her husband back for her education obtained while married, as well as the bride price her husband paid—plus interest. Nira is aware of this and still stands true to her heart. Dympna, staying true to her culture, condemns Nira for her behavior, and their friendship disintegrates. Finally Dympna resents, and is apathetic to, Nira's needs, and mourns her Americanization.

Although this is not a news story, it comments on an interesting insight into the Americanization of other cultures. It is intriguing to see people from other countries and ways of life integrate into American culture—some retaining their culture, others defying their people and assimilating into American society. Many of us are unaware of these peoples' traditions' being kept alive in spite of the environment around them. More than ever, people from all over the world come to the United States and acclimate to our way of life. Both the internal and external conflict of breaking apart from a rooted heritage so one can conform to a new culture and environment must be a tremendous [strain] for some folks. For others, I'm sure it is enlightening. The question is, whether it is the conscious choice or a transcendence of moral and traditional sensibilities that interests me about this story. I found it most interesting due to its unforgiving point of view from the Nigerian writer and the unfaltering attitude of the friend who finds she must follow her heart instead of her heritage.

Everywhere people are migrating and having to face the puzzle of their own identity, now that they live within a new context. What is me, what is my conditioning, and what is culturally transmitted? What can I choose to change? And if I try to let go of my culture, will I lose "me"?

As a transplant myself, I like how Michelle's version leaves this ambiguous. Does Nira consciously choose a life that gives more autonomy to women, or does she, by adjusting to her new cultural surroundings, unconsciously negate her ethnic values? The moral starkness of the story and the way that nobody wins feels true to life.

The organization of the narrative displays a range of antithetical relationship: between Ibo woman and Ibo man; between the woman and her female friends; and between one woman and her Ibo culture versus the other woman and her adopted American culture.

Each new dialectic reveals further conflicts in the central character. Since the film is about Nira's changing attitudes and beliefs, the story should be constructed to show the gradual transition in Nira until she makes the decision to go against the Ibo grain. This would allow the audience to sense not only the contrasting emotions and interactions of those closest to Nira, but those in Nira as well.

I would advise dumping the heavy reliance on phone calls, which points backward to the story's literary roots. Phone conversations tend to be flat in movies, because they narrate rather than dramatize.

The film could start with Nira's voice-over describing to someone how she was before she became Americanized. This would allow a transition into scenes of Nira with her family during a meal, a small evening get-together of close Ibo friends—with cuts to the room in which the men interact, along with a longer, more in-depth segment of the women's conversation in the kitchen, and then a moment when they all are together. Showing traditional celebrations and close-ups of Nira would fill the middle of the film and express Nira's growing sense of incongruity with her family role. It would also be necessary to show Nira away from her family and in the cultural environment at her place of work, and in other non-Ibo environments, to contrast her cultural ties.

Toward the end of the film, we might have cuts from Nira to Dympna on the phone with Nira trying to communicate her feelings, intercut with an interview scene where Nira is alone in the frame, talking to an unknown person. This would leave the audience feeling more closely tied to the overall narration of the film and alleviate any American or Nigerian partiality.

This idea is an original and imaginative bid to show how much danger, pain, and sacrifice result when a woman tries to appropriate more congenial cultural assumptions. The people who are supposed to value her withdraw their approval, but Nira seems ready for this and accepts the hard, lonely road of freedom. The idea itself comes from a Nigerian short story, and it inhabits a zone somewhere between fact and fiction. Michelle has treated it like a documentary, and there is much to suggest that its characters' authenticity would allow it to be made as a docudrama.

Its fidelity to its purpose, which is to show what happens when people respond to the host culture and abandon the precepts of their upbringings, gives it such moral integrity that it is almost irrelevant whether Dympna and Nira are actors or real characters. They are enacting dilemmas so profound and authentic to the immigrant's condition that we cannot fail to take them seriously. Nira wants the kind of personal identity she sees in American women, and her need is so compelling that she is ready to forfeit children, home, money, and family. She compels our respect by being ready to jettison all that previously made life worth living, in exchange for an identity that she determines herself. Sadly, her best friend cannot accompany her along this path and must abandon her too. To take a single step in Nira's direction would invite becoming an outcast, since in the story's version of Ibo relationships, "all is well" only when everyone keeps their place. Since all traditional cultures, including fundamentalist American ones, prescribe a hierarchy or division of labor along gender lines, this gives the story universal resonance.

In spite of Michelle's evenhanded treatment, the two women cannot be of equal weight. Nira is the central character, because she risks everything to make a change in her life, and she loses or gains (depending on one's point of view) everything that is supposed to matter. She develops, Dympna does not.

Literature can be omniscient more easily than film, especially where characters' inner lives are concerned. The film version would be stronger if it showed not only the two women's lives but Ibo life in America through Nira's eyes. She, after all, is the one who perceives options and makes a choice. Her friend may see these options just as clearly, but she renounces their long friendship so she can stay within the circle of security. Unstated is a ticking time bomb: their children will all become assimilated, and then it will be Dympna, not Nira, who faces separation. Cultures, like rare plants and animals, usually cannot sustain themselves outside their primary environments.

Is this really a documentary? I want to give the benefit of the doubt. Michelle's version focuses on the imperatives of power and gender by which a culture sustains itself, not on the psychology of the individuals concerned. There is no display of individual emotion. Indeed, emotion plays little part in the characters' lives. All tread the paths of their destiny, except Nira, who chooses to change and elects to pay the price—without an ounce of sentimentality or regret.

The austerity of these lives and the starkness of their choices lends them grandeur. If the story were played by Ibos living in America, individuals also struggling with the pain of disparate roles, you would have a drama rooted in the actuality of actual Ibo lives—a representation with powerful documentary overtones.

DISCUSSION

All three documentary subjects are by women, and all concern themselves with family life and the fate that befalls anybody stepping beyond the circle of conformity. Number 1 is an "issue" documentary. Timmy hates school, but since this makes him abnormal, he is placed under the influence of people who intend to change him. The drug intended to normalize him seems to exhibit awful side-effects, and the boy gets spectacularly worse. Who or what is to blame when efforts to regulate backfire so badly?

Number 2 is an issue film too. Suicidal teens are passing through the age of greatest vulnerability. Feeling like outcasts, some prefer to kill themselves (and since the Columbine High School massacres, their enemies) rather than continue living among those whom they feel do not value them. Cynthia's film deals with the despair but not the anger that's implied in the act, an anger that makes its finality so hard to bear for the survivors.

Number 3, though character driven rather than subject driven, also centers on the issue of identity and its cultural context. While Timmy and the suicidal teens are victims who cannot be said to understand their plight, Nira seems quite conscious (though not necessarily reflective) about what she is doing. She pays a high price willingly and resolutely, knowing that choosing autonomy means that she cannot be an Ibo mother. She is no misfit, blinded by pain and rage. Her eyes have been opened to the freer rules that govern other women's lives, and if she suffers it is because she cannot undo the knowledge.

Many documentaries are biographical, and thus character driven. All characters of any magnitude invariably have issues in their lives that arise from the imperatives of their temperaments. Character is fate, and showing a real character wrestling with his or her goals and demons can be a richly satisfying way to explore the nexus between disposition and destiny. It is also an elegantly displaced way to explore issues in the forefront of one's own life, a method that can be pursued without stepping in front of the camera oneself.

There are also:

- Event-driven documentaries, which chronicle an event and its effect on given characters.
- Diary documentaries, in which the camera is used as a notebook.
- Essay documentaries, which do what a photo or literary essay might.
- Historical documentaries.
- Travelogue documentaries.
- Journey or process documentaries.
- Reflexive documentaries, which reflect on the effects of the making of the film or on the process of the filmmakers.
- Fake documentaries ("mockumentaries") that properly lampoon the clichés and earnestness of the worst forms. There's something for everybody!

GOING FARTHER

If documentary or docudrama calls to you, here is more how-to guidance.

Rabiger, Michael. *Directing the Documentary*, 3d ed. Boston: Focal Press, 1998. (Deals with the whole process, from research through all the procedures and conceptual/aesthetic dilemmas on the way to the final edited version. Contains an extensive bibliography.)

Rosenthal, Alan. *Why Docudrama? Fact-Fiction on Film and TV*. Carbondale, IL: Southern Illinois University Press, 1999. (An anthology of essays about the history, practice, and problems of docudrama.)

Rosenthal, Alan. *Writing Docudrama: Dramatizing Reality for Film and TV*. Boston: Focal Press, 1994. (This is devoted to the problems and advantages of the hybrid form. From concept to completion, a thorough, down-to-earth grasp of all the ins and outs of writing the docudrama. Explains how to: find and research ideas; develop them into viable stories; use dialogue to shape characters; and progress from a treatment to a saleable script. Also includes a chapter on the responsibilities involved with mixing truth and fiction.)

14

Thirty-Minute Original Fiction

Short fiction films have the same challenges and rewards as short stories. Both demand a plot, developed characters, interesting situations, and a substantial thematic purpose—for no matter how short the film or ingenious its conception, it will waste its audience's time unless it has something arresting to say about the human condition. A short fiction film is therefore a full test of dramatic capability, in a limited compass.

> *Authorial point of view.* A singular point of view on the human condition in your stories will give them vitality.

Short literary or screen drama usually has these characteristics in common:

- It rapidly and economically sets up a main character and his or her world.
- The main character is in a special set of circumstances.
- He or she has something particular to accomplish, get, or do.
- How he or she handles key difficulties or impediments enlarges our sense of his/her issues, vulnerability, and capacities.
- The main character is often pushed to some boundary where he or she must take action.
- This action provokes a new awareness of the need to learn and develop, either in the audience or in the character.
- Ultimately, even if we learn, the main character may not. Not all stories are about winners.

This list is less a formula than a roundup of how effective storytellers exploit their limited time with an audience. Why do these elements so often appear? Probably because we are always looking for good stories, and we want to care about the central character. Though many stories end unhappily, we still hope along the way that the main character learns and grows in some way, and we recognize that unhappy endings are as true as happy ones. Behind these impulses lies an ancient and unchanging human need that stories help to answer. As Michael Roemer says in *Telling Stories*,[1]

> The connection between story, or myth, and ritual has long been noted and debated. Ritual too constitutes a safe arena in which we can encounter the sacred or "real," acknowledge our helplessness and limitations, abandon our weapons and defenses, surrender control, forgive others, and be ourselves forgiven. Both ritual and plot conjugate the particular to the universal. Moreover, in ritual as in comedy and tragedy it is largely our fear, weakness, and failure— the very secrets that keep us apart in daily life—that bring us together.

Good storytelling does a lot more than offer diversion. So often it invokes the troubling forces in our lives—forces such as morality, the contradictions in being human, and the implacable laws of the universe—and helps us live with them both as individuals and as members of society. This remains true even when the characters themselves seem light or amoral.

ASSIGNMENT

Treatment for An Original Thirty-Minute Fiction Piece

Write an original fiction film treatment centering around one character. We should be led to understand his or her subjective point of view, though not necessarily to agree with or like it. Try to base the story on something you have closely observed or lived through, but *avoid fictionalizing something you experienced directly yourself*, since this will push you into the mold of disguised diary writing, with all the attendant questions of fidelity to the original events. Your presentation should include:

1. A scene outline summarizing the story
2. A "shopping list" of the sequences with their intended running times. Estimate running times by acting out each sequence as you time it, playing all the parts yourself, and visualizing each shot (but warn those in earshot or risk being carted away in the rubber bus).

Analysis

Define the story's underlying meaning and purpose.

1. Michael Roemer, *Telling Stories: Postmodernism and the Invalidation of Traditional Narrative*. Lanham, MD: Rowman & Littlefield, 1995.

EXAMPLES

Example 1: Thirty-Minute Original Fiction Idea
(Michael Hanttula)

Scene Outline.   It is the forced-retirement day for the president of a major, but anonymous, corporation. Many people, especially a team of vice-presidents, are set to gain from the president's retirement. However, he has refused to comply and has turned his office into a bunker where he has been fending off would-be intruders, slaying anyone making an attempt to oust him from his position. One by one, lower-ranking employees have made their way up to the top floor and tried to charge his makeshift bunker. Each time, they are terribly wounded or, in some way, incapacitated. Over time, the vice-presidents have run out of secretaries, assistants, and coffee people to send. Before giving up, they remember Farrago, the mailroom boy in the basement.

They send a message down to tell him that his assistance is greatly needed and that his help will undoubtedly result in the grand promotion he has been hoping for. Farrago hurries up to the lobby of the building, where the vice-presidents and heads-of-departments have established a headquarters. Tables are overturned, facing a bank of elevators on the far wall. People are busy scurrying around, looking over reports, yelling into communication devices, plotting maps and missions.

The main vice-president quickly briefs Farrago on the situation, telling of the evil actions by the president and the severity of [the need to remove] him from office. As she does this, one of the elevator doors makes a beeping sound and begins to open. Everyone dives for cover behind the tables. A secretary slowly crawls out of the elevator on his hands and knees. Many people rush to his assistance. He is clearly dying of undefined wounds. In his last breaths he is able to give the latest position of the president and warns that it will be impossible to take over the president's stronghold. He dies and Farrago becomes discouraged. However, the head vice-president reminds him of the promotion that will be his if he can dethrone the president. He agrees to the mission, collects supplies and maps, and heads up the towering building by elevator.

Inside the elevator Farrago dreams of the power and prestige his promotion will bring him as he is hailed slayer of the president by the rest of the staff. On the top floor, he gets out and finds a labyrinth of office cubicles before him. He searches through the maze, running into dead ends, fallen adversaries that have attempted this mission before him, and various traps that impede his journey.

Along the way he runs into a guard who has decided to protect the president. They get into a scuffle and the guard is close to winning. But Farrago manages to escape the guard's grasp and, fleeing back into the labyrinth, stops short of one of the traps and takes refuge down another corridor. The guard, in fast pursuit, barrels around the corner, flings himself into the trap. As Farrago closes in to finish off the guard, he discovers that the guard is himself. He stops, the guard begs him to help the president—praising the president's goodness and condemning the evil staff that has been trying to usurp him. [The guard dies.]

Farrago, now quite confused, travels further into the labyrinth after the guard's death, still in search of the president. Eventually, he happens upon his office and finds the president looking out of the window. He is aware of Farrago's presence, but not taking action.

The president states what Farrago is here for and simply asks that certain affairs [be] taken care of by the corporation after he is gone. The president tells of his initial hopes for the company and how he had wanted to do so much good. But when he tried, his staff revolted and have [since] been trying to get him out.

These are surprisingly humane desires for someone that has been declared a "villain of the people" by his staff. Farrago looks about the office, seeing awards and letters of gratitude from charities and other signs of his "good deeds." The words of the head vice-president and of the loyal guard echo through his head. The president knows about the offers of promotion that his staff will have made to Farrago and agrees that this is the best way for him to advance. However, Farrago's dream of the life of luxury that promotion offers is darkened by visions of the type of person he would become (like the staff is now) if he had such power. He moves towards the president, drawing the weapon that the staff gave him.

Back in the staff's headquarters, many are waiting anxiously, while others are still in a great deal of commotion (making deals with other companies, assuring [them] that the president is being replaced). The elevator begins its descent from the top floor and the tension in the control room becomes greater with each floor the elevator descends. Eventually, it reaches the ground floor and the elevator bell rings, the doors burst open, and Farrago and the president come charging out together.

Meaning/Purpose of the Story.   This story is about the corruption of power and the struggle to do good. Farrago first wants his promotion and will do what is necessary to get it, without thinking of the actions he'll have to take. He is, at first, manipulated by the staff with promises of promotion and power. Then, as he searches for the president, he is confronted by the guard who stops him and makes him think about what he is doing. By the time he gets to the president, he sees that the president is a person much like anyone else and that he is not the monster that the staff has described. Farrago's eagerness to aid the vice-presidents' struggle against the "dictator" president is vanquished and he sees that the president is the one with the more appealing morals. However, he realizes that if he helps the president, his opportunities for promotion would be lost. His greatest decision is between the struggle for advancing his career and his struggle for being a good person. In the end, he chooses to side with the president in an uncertain battle against the forces of the staff.

Shopping List of Sequences
1. Photomontage under titles of actions occurring in the headquarters. Use of voice-over and sound design to give the backstory (previous attempts to usurp the president, staff's decision to call upon the mailroom attendant)—forty-five seconds.
2. Farrago in mailroom (basement) amidst piles and piles of unsorted mail, working diligently, message drops from above with request to come above and see vice-presidents about a promotion—forty-five seconds.
3. Farrago entering the lobby/headquarters, being briefed, witnessing failed attempt emerging from elevator, agreeing to go, being sent up the elevator—four minutes.
4. Farrago in elevator, dreaming of his prosperous future. He is shaken out of dream when elevator arrives on the top floor—thirty seconds.
5. He sees the labyrinth before him and begins to proceed through it. He runs into dead ends, dead secretaries, and pitfalls—two minutes.
6. He runs into guard, battles, flees, hides, guard is injured, they talk, Farrago continues on—three minutes.

7. He finds president, enters his office, and listens to his story. He dreams [about the choice] between the "good life" and leading a "good" life. He makes his decision—four minutes.
8. Farrago and the president return to the lobby, surprising the staff, they attack—one minute.

Total approximate time: sixteen minutes.

This is delightful Monty Pythonesque comedy, but even comedy, as we shall see, conforms to dramatic norms if it is to work well. Each genre—whether farce, comedy *noir*, screwball comedy, historical fiction, buddy movie, or psychological thriller—comes with a set of audience expectations that the artist may both use and constructively subvert.

> Every *genre* has its conventions, which are both useful and confining. These establish a rapport with the audience but always threaten to make the piece predictable. Anything of excellence will often subvert, and therefore challenge, what is standard.

Michael's sequences, though likely to run longer than his estimated times, probably still fall short of the intended thirty-minute length, so the piece unquestionably needs developing from the point of screen time alone. The situation outlined at the beginning, of the underlings being sent up one by one to capture the president, seems too important, and potentially too richly comic, to be consigned to backstory status. I would advise that we enter the story at an earlier stage, when our hero in his basement mailroom is still obscure.

From this point on there are some story elements missing. Whenever you feel this, try uncovering hidden potential by rendering the story into its closest mythical, legendary, or historical equivalent. This reveals archetypal parallels. We see that the corporation is a kingdom, and the president its king. The building is his castle, and he is under siege and about to be deposed by his barons.

Familiar in every national or group history is the situation where the lame-duck leader slips from power, eclipsed through age, sickness, fatal mistakes, or (as here) because his term is up. The ambitious begin jostling for new positions in the hierarchy, and the body politic becomes unstable. This corporate leader has grown fond of power and won't step down. Being at the top of the building, able to see over the kingdom, he is sequestered and poorly known to his inferiors. Now they want his power for themselves.

In Michael's story, Farrago is the lowly page or kitchen boy of folk tales pressed into service when everyone else has failed. Though Farrago's willingness to follow orders could be simpleminded loyalty, it comes in fact from ambition. He dreams of self-advancement in one leap rather than by inching up the career ladder. Because this motive is specious, he could be naïve—or he could be opportunistic, like the VPs in the lobby, who have cannily expended their underlings in battle, not risking themselves. This moral ambiguity is useful, because it makes Farrago less predictable. Starting out as an amoral Everyman, he doesn't deserve to triumph. In fact, the longer the story can keep the odds stacked against him, the longer the outcome generates doubt and dramatic tension.

> *The uses of delay.* The father of the mystery novel, Wilkie Collins, advocated delay in storytelling as a way of holding the reader's attention: "Make them laugh, make them cry, but make them wait."

Once Farrago has glimpsed his reward, he goes into the labyrinth, with its traps, vanquished fighters, and guardian. Finding the way through, he faces what every labyrinth needs—a minotaur, in the shape of the guard.

Farrago has so far faced an elaborate testing of his luck, ingenuity, and persistence. Now he must confront the guardian of the inner sanctum. On passing this test too, he wins information (that the president is really a good person), which he seems to accept at face value. This is problematical, for it kills any further dramatic tension. It also prevents him from making the discovery himself.

The other big problem is that the guard "is himself." Were this reflexive identity built into the fabric of the whole piece, it could be fascinating, but it isn't followed up or used later (by Farrago finding that the president too is himself, for example). A single occurrence is inconsistent and misleading, so I would recommend dropping it. Instead, I suggest playing the scene so the guard appears to use his dying breath to set up Farrago for another, bigger trap.

The guard is a "shapeshifter," for he appears as a defender and opponent yet turns out to be a helper. Farrago cannot be sure of this and sensibly takes him for a "trickster." Now, as Farrago prepares to enter the ultimate sanctum, he should approach the inner office as if nearing the seat of an evil empire. To heighten the tension, he should move through a series of situations that seem calculated to destroy him, as in the sequence when Dorothy and her friends arrive at the fearful Wizard of Oz's castle. Farrago eventually finds the president, apparently undefended. This can be a sequence of great tension as we wait for the lightning bolt that will destroy Farrago.

When the president claims to be a good person, Farrago should not immediately decide that he and all

> *Archetypes.* Among all the archetypal roles, such as Hero, Antagonist, Mentor, and Guardian, the Shapeshifter, Trickster, and Shadow are the most complex and interesting types. The Shapeshifter contributes suspense by being changeable or unreliable. The Trickster is often a comic figure but can plot the hero's undoing. The Shadow epitomizes the demons and other dark, repressed forces that the hero (or heroine, of course) must face.

his "good works" paraphernalia should be taken at face value. To keep us in suspense, Farrago should interrogate the president, perhaps to find out how the stand-off developed and why he won't resign. Here Farrago, like Faust, might bargain for his future with the devil incarnate. Our hero is trying to persuade himself that the president is a misunderstood man. Is he in worse danger for believing this?

If Michael's ending—Farrago emerging from the elevator in cahoots with the embattled president—is to remain viable, Farrago's options must remain ambiguous right up to the point where the elevator door opens and they emerge as gunslinging partners. But this seems like a trick ending; it lacks substance. What in fact will the partners do as they confront the VPs, either for themselves or for the corporation? If outgunned, will they die in a *Bonnie and Clyde* shoot-out? The president could still, in a plot-point moment, reveal his true nature and grab the gullible Farrago as a human shield.

However, if their partnership is genuine and their motives good, they must somehow outwit the VPs and reinstall a benevolent leadership. A happy ending is expected of broad comedy, but the unresolved nature of this ending leaves a nagging question: how can a good man overstay his allotted time and remain admirable?

The minor characters might need developing, if most of the employees are to be talked into reinstalling the old president. This is difficult to imagine, since all the lower-level employees have died, leaving only the greedy middle-management types. When all the decent guys have fallen in battle, it rather strains credibility to make the bad guys go through a conversion. Even in comedy, life is seldom like that.

An alternative ending would be for Farrago and the president to contrive an escape. We might see them running off into the sunset to start a new company somewhere else. Though this is true to comedy's happy endings, it violates one of the piece's central assumptions—that the corporation headquarters is an enclosed world in which fighting is to the death.

In summary, Farrago's journey from the basement up to the lobby, and his briefing for his heroic journey, are viable as they stand. But his journey through the labyrinth needs building up, and the guard even in death needs to be more ambiguous. The ordeal in the president's office needs to have many more steps and be made fraught with tension and uncertainty, particularly as the president seems to reveal a quiet goodness. The denouement in the lobby needs reworking. Were enough proletarians left alive in the lobby for Farrago to persuade, he could conceivably become a counterrevolutionary who turns the tables on an evil middle-management.

My suggestions amount to raising the stakes for Farrago, giving him more to contest, more obstacles to get past, and more dif-

> *Raising the stakes.* Frequently in a story's development the main character is not given enough to fight for. A skilled storyteller raises the stakes as high as possible without violating the story's credibility.

ficult choices to make. This represents a lot of development and will easily expand the story to fill thirty minutes.

Example 2: "Eggs Benedict" (Michelle Arnove)

Summary.   "Eggs Benedict" is a bittersweet comedy about a struggling student, Meg Benedict. Under severe financial difficulties she goes to a fertility center and donates one of her eggs to the bank in exchange for funds.

A young couple, Kevin and Mary Donovan, who are having difficulty becoming pregnant, visit the fertility center and opt to go the route of artificial insemination, hence Meg's egg. Two years later all is well until Mary is tragically killed in a terrible auto accident. Kevin is devastated, but is showered with love and affection by his family and friends who try to help him overcome his deep sorrow. Approximately three years later, Kevin becomes obsessed with thoughts of the semi-biological mother of his child and sets out to locate her. Through a series of channels, he is led to Meg and finds her single, attractive and not interested in anything other than her hard-hitting career in journalism. His intentions are not initially romantic, but after he meets up with Meg, he is overcome with attraction and lust. Confused and afraid, he manages to befriend her, but under false pretenses. It is not until after a few encounters that Kevin discloses his real reasons for pursuing Meg—leaving her at first angry and confused, then finally enchanted by Kevin and the baby. The rest is history. . . .

Meaning/Purpose of the Story.   The story's underlying meaning and purpose suggest, again, destiny and the idea that life and death are cyclical. Although Mary's death is tragic, the birth of the baby and the eventual meeting of Kevin and Meg are inevitable. While their meeting is not accidental, the events that lead up to it suggest a sort of fate, and this lends an enlightening feeling that "accidents" and the unexpected don't always mean a truly negative outcome.

Shopping List of Sequences
1. INT. MEG'S APARTMENT: Meg is preoccupied with worries. She locates articles from magazines describing fertility clinic and egg donation—seven minutes.

2. EXT. FERTILITY CLINIC: Meg hesitates entering clinic—two minutes.
3. INT. CLINIC: As Meg is leaving, she passes Kevin and Mary in lobby, however neither party sees the other—two minutes.

"TWO YEARS LATER"

4. MARY LEAVES HOUSE—one minute.
5. MARY'S CAR ACCIDENT—one minute.
6. INT. KEVIN AND MARY'S HOME: Kevin is in mourning—two minutes.
7. INT. MEG'S OFFICE: Meg gets phone call regarding a tip on a great story—two minutes.
8. EXT. OUTDOOR CAFE: Meg meets Kevin—three minutes.
9. EXT. MONTAGES: Kevin and Meg walk the city, have dinner, take a drive together—six minutes.
10. INT. KEVIN'S HOME: Kevin writes a letter to Meg—two minutes.
11. EXT. MEG'S FRONT DOOR: Kevin arrives and Meg greets him with affection—two minutes.

Overall approximate total: thirty minutes.

Here's another comedy. The materials are quite sketchy, especially the sequence list, where Michelle leaves out the all-important baby material. But the writing is very promising, and this I think comes from the heartfelt comments she makes on the story's underlying philosophy. She believes that life is cyclical, that Fate practices a rough justice: what is taken away in one place will be given back in another. Comedy is a good vehicle for this.

Not for nothing does Michelle describe it as a bittersweet comedy, for she kills off one of her main characters rather early. For me, at least, there are a couple of problems with this. It is suspiciously coincidental; it looks a little too much like the author cranking up the pressure on Kevin. A death in a romantic comedy has its risks, but this would hardly be the first time it's been done. George in a *Seinfeld* episode managed inadvertently to *kill* his fiancée, and the audience found it hilarious. Does this depend on values built up during a whole series? I don't know.

For my taste, I would advise seeking the same effect using less extreme means. Maybe make Mary flighty from the beginning—she might go back to her first love, leaving Kevin holding the baby that he had thought would keep them together. By making her exit into a character issue, the story can avoid an awkward transition and let Kevin first process Mary's absence before getting curious about his child's biological mother. He would need to go through these stages creditably if we are to preserve our interest and belief in him. But is it necessary, in order to make Kevin a person of worth, to accompany him through all five Kubler-Ross stages of loss? Unless they could all be funny, this would hold up the story's central purpose, which is to send a single father out to find, and then court, the initially resistant mother of his child.

The rest of Michelle's movie has no insuperable difficulties. It's really a variation on the chase or hunt movie, with the quarry in control and the hunter having to use charm, ingenuity, and a secret weapon (their baby, and its potential effect on Meg's submerged motherly instincts) for the final assault.

One of the story's purposes must be to put Meg's identity as an independent-minded feminist under stress by facing her with the primal lure of motherhood. Kevin uses their baby as a trojan horse in order to undermine Meg's ambitions. Before she knows what has hit her, she has to decide between her head and her heart, between her career in journalism and her fascination with her child. The catch is that she cannot have her child unless she takes its father and becomes part of a family—another of life's challenges and compromises.

Now that we see where the story wants to go, we can speculate about what else it needs. The first phase is to build up the pressures on the main characters and thus fill them out as they react under duress. Meg needs to survive economically in order to achieve her promising career. We know how much it matters from her having done something so extreme—selling a part of her own body and lineage. Kevin and Mary need a child, but if Mary is to be eliminated, it must be handled with some delicacy so the story doesn't shoot itself in the foot. In life, one partner might think that having a child will hold the marriage together. When Mary leaves anyway, Kevin is left literally holding the baby, and his primal need for a mate makes him seek the child's biological mother.

> *Every story, like every person, has its own identity.* You have to give birth to a story before you can see what it is and where it wants to go. Serving the tale, doing its bidding, is one of the secret pleasures of authorship.

Kevin's needs are clearly defined throughout, and what's delightful is that Michelle has turned the gender tables by making Kevin the compulsive nest builder. It is Kevin who must attempt to corral Meg, and Meg must resist mightily. That's the satisfaction of this piece. Though its outcome is almost inevitable, the author must keep us (and Kevin) guessing as long as possible. She could make Meg a promising journalist who is following the story of her career. Kevin could feel he must hide their baby, in the mistaken idea that it will alienate her. Maybe Meg, in writing up her story, declares feminist principles or ideas that make Kevin's plans seem hopeless. Not only must the duel between their conflicting needs be kept up, but it must be escalated to the movie's major crisis point—where Meg realizes that Kevin's baby is also hers.

To raise the stakes, Meg's important story might be about surrogate parenthood, and it would be a delightful irony if her journalism led her to discover that the baby of the man who so relentlessly follows her is actually hers too. This offers wonderfully serpentine plot possibilities, with the charm of the baby's ultimately disarming Meg and compelling her to make an about-turn.

> *Plot* is the container that shapes each incident, and its scenes form the chain of cause and effect that demonstrates how the central character encounters antagonistic forces and then struggles with them. Getting every scene to follow inevitably from the last takes a great deal of work.

If Mary is absent instead of dead, another irony is possible. After Meg and Kevin have come together, Mary could return, only to find she has lost her place as Kevin's wife. The final question is, can Kevin and Meg be large hearted enough to accommodate her late desire to see the child they have all three made together? Now you have a modern romance, one that could only happen after doctors made parenthood triangular.

In the end, we must ask whether Kevin loves either woman or is acting out biological urges to build a home and family. If everyone is happy, the story asks, does "love" actually matter in the end? This reminds us of ancient practices of arranged marriage, where a culture puts building families ahead of the unreliable precepts of romance. Marriage based on shared and practical needs is thousands of years old, while romantic marriage is recent, beginning in the Middle Ages with the notion of courtly love. Made into wonderful Arthurian narratives by troubadours, these traditions have been carried on faithfully by Hollywood to this day.

By implying that the family is more important and durable than romance, Michelle might boldly challenge a seven-hundred-year-old fad.

> *Willpower.* The powerhouse in all drama, whether it be comedy, tragedy, or anything else, is the will of the main characters to get or do what matters to them.

DISCUSSION

Michael's story about the postal clerk Farrago has one point-of-view character, while Michelle's tale unintentionally anticipates the next chapter's assignment by having two, neither of whom having a predominating point of view.

From the commentary these stories have generated you can see that comedy depends on the same underlying motivations as tragedy or any other genre. There must be risks and dangers for the characters if they are to struggle meaningfully for what they want or believe in.

Ultimately every story, no matter what form of representation it takes, depends for its continuation and success on maintaining a balance of human and natural forces. Most story-development effort is expended on getting these forces right, with respect to their identity, motives, balance, and outcome. Without a proper balance of forces, the audience knows that the central situation would do a nosedive. Farrago would be unequal to his mission, or Kevin would decide that courting Meg is a losing proposition—end of story.

Developing a story is really the task of extending or adjusting each situation so it first maintains its tension, then resolves into another, and yet another. You will go through many, many drafts before you and your demanding (one hopes) readers agree that the piece is "there."

This is fascinating, exacting, and ultimately tremendously fulfilling work. As your piece really begins to make sense throughout, you will

> *Really get to know your characters and their world.* Many fiction films fail because the key players—writer, director, and actors—have not engaged in a full development process. Extensive story development first, and exploratory rehearsals later, allow everyone to become truly intimate with the characters and their story. When all this happens, it really shows.

feel the thrill of doing a demanding job well. Now at last you have a strong blueprint to follow in making a film. In fiction this is three-quarters of the battle, and in comedy it is nine-tenths.

The development process of a successful thirty-minute film can take months of regular, concerted effort that extends into fifteen or twenty drafts. By then you will have come to know your characters and their world thoroughly, something you realize you didn't at all during the early stages. This is a prerequisite for anyone proposing to direct a movie intelligently and authoritatively. If you are a beginner and lack experience, this is all the more true. Making films is like making chains with a thousand links. Beginner's luck never applies; beginner's hard work is something different.

GOING FARTHER

Cooper, Pat, and Ken Dancyger. *Writing the Short Film.* 2nd ed. Boston: Focal Press, 2000. (Like poetry in relation to prose, the short form presents more difficulties than the long one, and this book helps you grapple with the problems. Its explication of dramatic concepts will make a useful alternative to mine.)

Dancyger, Ken, and Jeff Rush. *Alternative Scriptwriting: Writing beyond the Rules.* Boston: Focal Press, 1995. (Explores variations of what is possible in the nontraditional short form and includes counterstructure, working with and against genre, character distinctions and limits, character-driven as opposed to plot-driven drama, tone and "the inescapability of irony," and writing samples.)

Rabiger, Michael. *Directing: Film Techniques and Aesthetics*, 2d ed. Boston: Focal Press, 1997. (Teaches the essentials of the entire fiction filmmaking process, including writing from the viewpoint of actor, director, and screenwriter. The sections of the book on how actors control the inner lives of their characters will be specially interesting.)

---15---

Feature Film

Everyone dreams of writing a successful feature film, but this is a tall order even in bare outline form. To satisfy an audience takes richly detailed characters, a plot covering a plethora of events, and themes with depth. In fact, writing a feature film takes almost as much work, narrative material, and thematic depth as a novel.

In this chapter we can only go to the foot of the mountain, since even for professionals, developing a full screenplay may take twenty drafts and months or years of work. However, the initial outline is the most significant and exciting part, and that's what we are going to do.

> *"Nothing human is alien to me"* (Terence, c.195–159 B.C.). Being the center of the universe is so familiar from childhood that most people first write fiction as a cover for autobiography. More difficult but rewarding is to break out of the prison of Self and direct one's efforts at creating the lives of people unlike oneself. This may start from the intellect, but with practice your heart will catch up with your head.

ASSIGNMENT

Write *a feature film idea using two main points of view.* Where the thirty-minute original fiction project let you concentrate on exploring the experience of one character, this one requires that you profile with equal sympathy the quests and development of two. You will need to build considerable potential for development into the characters and their

> *Round and flat characters.* E. M. Forster divided fictional characters into two kinds. Round characters are fully realized psychological portraits; flat characters lack depth and often exist to serve a minor purpose. Advanced writers can people a work with round characters, because they have developed the imagination to enter other people's realities.

situations. Another aim is to get your audience interested in, and sympathetic to, at least one point of view to which you are temperamentally opposed. This requires that the writer *no longer identify exclusively with one character*. Instead, one must be able to create each character's situation somewhat objectively from the outside but also to inhabit each main character's perceptions, which may be imperfect or even odious, from the inside. For your presentation, write:

1. A treatment outline.
2. A definition of the themes being handled by the story.
3. A "shopping list" of sequences and their approximate timings, which should add up to about ninety minutes.

EXAMPLES

Example 1: Feature Film Idea (Paul Flanagan)

Treatment Outline.   Henry, a hefty 19 year old tobacco farmer, and John, a 21 year old loner, stand before the Colonel inside a tent in Delaware. They have just joined the United States army in hope of assisting the American Revolution. They stand at attention as the Colonel sits behind his desk and begins to speak. He talks to them about the tough times that lie ahead, and the state of affairs in the rebellion. It is December 29, and General George Washington and his troops are suffering bitterly in their encampment in Valley Forge, Pennsylvania. They are freezing, have minimal food, and practically no clothes. They are also without their flag, for it was lost during a scuffle in Brandywine. Due to its utmost importance, the colonel instructs Henry and John to deliver the flag to Washington in Valley Forge. The soldiers stand motionless as the Colonel dismisses them.

John and Henry are in their tent packing their belongings. John clearly doesn't want the mission. It doesn't involve battle. Henry isn't crazy about it either but he knows his time to fight will come, and he might as well follow orders.

The boys arrive in Philadelphia, and walk through the city. John, completely lost, follows Henry, who seems to know his way around. The busy streets and vendors hurry them along as they scoot around a corner and arrive at their destination.

The two boys stand firmly in a very prim and proper home. Everything is polished clean and in its proper place. An elderly woman, Betsy Ross, appears with a folded American flag in her hand. They exchange some pleasant conversation, Henry throws the flag into a satchel, and they politely leave.

With the flag in their possession, Henry and John make their way out of the city and into the vast countryside ahead. They walk along for what seems like hours; talking to each other and trying to keep up enthusiasm. Henry walks while slowly slinging the satchel by his side, once bumping it into a tree and not taking notice.

They arrive at a large creek and stop at its edge. John knowing that they must go across reluctantly begins walking through the waist-high water. Upset at having to get wet, he makes his way across as quickly as possible. Henry follows, yelling at John for taking him through the water.

Once through, Henry questions John's navigational skills and they argue. Exhausted, they make camp for the night. Henry sitting close to the fire heats some food while John paces around the area. Henry, not being able to get comfortable, uses the satchel as a seat cushion. With the food cooked, John sits down and joins him. They eat their food and cover themselves as warmly as they can for the night.

Awake at the crack of dawn, John pops up. He scopes the area looking for their direction of travel. Uh oh! They've been going the wrong way. He wakes Henry, and John, now carrying the flag, is not any more protective of it. They climb hills, move through ditches and more creeks, until John finally collapses. To hell with this! And John tosses the satchel away. They've been tearing themselves up. John doesn't move from the ground. He's too numb from the cold and just doesn't give a damn. Two good men wasted on a stupid delivery mission. Henry picks up the flag, keeping their orders in mind, but sits down also. A moment passes as they can barely control their shivering. Uh! What was that? Redcoats! John and Henry stagger to their feet and take off. In thick woods, they are stumbling over just about everything. Whack! John runs into a branch. They keep running with their muskets at the ready. John is shot in the arm from behind. He falls. No use. They are surrounded.

Captured. They are beaten up, harassed, and taken away after a few minutes to a small British camp. They practically walked right into it. Tied to two trees, the boys are thoroughly questioned by one of the commanders as to the whereabouts of Washington. They keep their mouths shut.

Their muskets and gear have been stripped from them and laid to the side. The men go through the soldiers' belongings and find the flag. All hell breaks loose as the men tauntingly hold up the flag, swirl and throw it around. One in particular wraps himself in it and rolls on the ground.

John and Henry, feeling something they haven't felt before, grapple with their ropes. Henry can almost get free, and he would, if only a soldier didn't coincidentally shove a musket at his knees. Eventually the mocking ends, the flag is dropped, and they are left for the night.

Night arrives and Henry breaks free and unties John. They grab the flag, any food they can find, and deftly flee. Scared, they run and run and run. John looks deathly ill from his arm. He can't even move it. They spend a freezing night awake up against a tree.

The next morning they slowly begin walking along. They come upon a log cabin secluded in the woods. Before they get to the front step, they have a musket pointed at their heads. It's a young woman, Clair. John shocked by the gun, starts dribbling tears down his cheeks. Seeing the wound, Clair lowers the musket and brings them inside.

The home is amply furnished, and in exquisite taste. There is an American flag in the background on the wall. Three young children, around 10 years old, surround the men. A not-as-tough-as-he-looks teenager is standing in the corner with a musket at his side.

Clair and the children tend to the wound and wrap both men in blankets. After a small meal, Henry and John explain what they are doing and what had happened. They learn that Washington and his troops passed by in the fall and that Clair actually met him. Seeing the soiled and bloody flag, Clair exchanges hers for theirs. If it's going to be taken to General Washington it must be clean.

At daybreak they leave. Henry helps John along. John babbles about being home, and how he wishes he could stay at Clair's.

Only slightly rejuvenated they trudge along. Snow begins falling, and after a few miles' walking it's near a foot deep. Able to go no further, they halt. At the edge of the Brandy-wine River they sit and freeze. Henry, spotting shelter across the river in what appears to be an overhanging rock, gets up. It's likely they'll die from the cold water, but it will definitely happen if they stay where there are. After a quick look of mutual despair, they begin crossing the fast-moving current. Half way through Henry falls. Struggling to his feet, he realizes that he doesn't have the satchel. It's being swept away by the current! Henry darts after it.

John gets to solid ground and runs along the side. Snow is coming down fast. Henry goes under. John can't find him.

He jumps in! Searching, reaching, reaching, he's got an arm. He swims and pulls. They pull up on the bank on the other side and get under the rock. Stretched out, they look at each other—motionless. Their belongings are lost. Their flag is gone. Near death and freezing, night comes.

John and Henry awaken on their backs. Wrapped in blankets they are being carried on stretchers. They were right outside Valley Forge and didn't know it.

The area looks like hell. People are freezing, dead, or dying. The two men are brought into the camp and into shelter. The troops watch in amazement as they see these two men who survived the past night carried in. The troops tend to Henry and John and both, almost frozen to death, pass out.

The next morning John wakes up with no one else around but Henry. He wakes him and they eat the food laid out for them. Neither talk. They didn't bring the flag. John gets up and walks to the opening of the tent. He stands there motionless. Henry notices a change in John and finally speaks. He makes his way over the sees what John is looking at. The men of Valley Forge have made their own flag—from the clothes off their backs.

A few of the themes being handled are:
- The boys' journey into manhood. The entire story is a symbol of this.
- Themes of hope and struggle. The boys are up against unbelievable odds and are struggling all the way. The troops of Valley Forge are also struggling, for they are suffering in one of the worst winters ever.
- The theme of hope is also present in that the troops made their own flag in the end, taking the clothes off their backs in order to have something to fight for.
- There are also themes of compassion—compassion that Clair has for them, and compassion they have for each other.

"Shopping List" of Sequences:
In the tent receiving orders—10 minutes.
Packing belongings and heading out of town—5 minutes.
Arriving in Philadelphia and getting the flag from Betsy Ross—10 minutes.
First day's journey into the woods. They cross the creek—15 minutes.
First night's camp. They cook food, argue, and shiver— 5 minutes.

They wake up and continue the second day. John is carrying the flag—5 minutes.
John stumbles and wants to give up—5 minutes.
Redcoat chase scene—5 minutes.
They are captured and taken back to the British camp. Entire camp scene—15 minutes.
They escape from the British—5 minutes.
Night camp—5 minutes.
They arrive at Clair's home and are taken in—10 minutes.
They leave and lose the flag in the river—10 minutes.
They are taken into Valley Forge and are tended to—10 minutes.
They wake up the next morning and see the handmade flag—5 minutes.
Total minutes—120

The strength of this idea is that it chronicles a journey, a test given to two immature men, who must accomplish something holding great symbolic importance for them. Like their own emerging nation, these untried, rural partners must pass through trials, hardships, and disappointments on their way toward adult maturity and knowledge.

A powerful tool for clarifying each scene is to see how many vital questions it raises. This turns a scene from being informative (and undramatic) into the more dramatic condition of evoking dilemmas. The *tests* that John and Henry must pass are full of such dilemmas:

> *Drama poses questions.* Good drama artfully involves us with characters' predicaments so that we come to care how they tackle their problems. Every major scene should evoke questions, and as we look for answers, it charges us up with anticipation for the next scene. Drama's job is not to inform but to teach inductively, by inviting us to exercise our faculties, which we can then use better during crises in our own lives.

1. *Manners*—can these country bumpkins behave properly in a lady's living room, and can they make their way through the big city?
2. *Endurance*—can they handle the endless trek through the countryside, especially once soaked and freezing from crossing the creek?
3. *Cooperation*—can they agree about navigation and on the worth of their purpose?
4. *Ingenuity*—can they make a meal and improvise a modicum of comfort?
5. *Endurance*—will they persist with their mission once they become lost and exhausted?
6. *Loyalty*—under the British taunts and bullying, can they keep silent about Washington's whereabouts, especially as John is wounded and vulnerable?

7. *Ingenuity*—are they resourceful enough to escape from their uncouth captors?
8. *Endurance*—can their bodies and spirits survive the worsening cold, when John becomes so ill?
9. *Luck*—when they evade their pursuers, can they find a haven?
10. *Pride*—can John recover from the embarrassment of crying in front of a woman?
11. *Paradise lost*—can they leave Clair's sanctuary and return to the comfortless world of their mission, especially with John disintegrating emotionally?
12. *Endurance*—can they go through one more river, and a dangerous one, in the uncertain hope of shelter on the other side?
13. *Failure*—after they nearly die in the river and lose the precious flag, can they find any reason to go on?
14. *Grace*—can they overcome the disillusioning fact that their mission was never necessary?

Just as the sled "Rosebud" in *Citizen Kane* runs through the movie as a symbol of the newspaper magnate's childhood loss, this film has the hand-made American flag as its emblem. The sled embodied what Kane, with all his wealth and power, could never recapture, while here the flag is the handcrafted representation of incipient American statehood, pride, and independence. Once the colony can sever the umbilical to England, it can begin growing up.

A flag is naturally something young men will die for, so it is ironic that the flag in this story has a worse time than its handlers. It gets used as a cushion, is nearly abandoned, and is so badly muddied and bloodied that Clair must replace it. Later it is dese-

> *Symbols and emblems.* Once you grasp what your story is about, you can think about featuring symbols and emblems that are organic to the story. The existence of key objects and images will help to give visible form to important underlying ideas. In Steinbeck's *The Grapes of Wrath*, it is the unreliable, worn-out vehicles, loaded with indigent families and their belongings, that come to represent man's uncertain progress through misfortune.

crated by the enemy and ultimately lost in the river. This makes a telling point, for ironically, their suffering turns out to be needless. So necessary to the revolutionary soldiers was a flag that they sacrificed precious clothing to make one. We see that what must get through is the symbol's meaning, not an actual flag.

If the fortunes of the flag in this film are a strength, what are the weaknesses? Again it is apparent from the large time allotted to some of the sequences that there is insufficient material—either to fill up the time or to carry the thematic weight of a major screen work. If you doubt this, try sitting with your eyes closed for five minutes, imagining what might be on the screen for the first sequence (John and Henry getting their orders). Ten minutes, one cinema reel, is a huge lapse of cinematic time. The audience, from all other films they have ever watched, will expect this rather static, expositional scene to happen in a minute or two at most.

Tests and dramatic incident are *not* what is missing. What is absent is a pronounced and individual character for each of the two young men, and for the subsidiary characters they encounter, particularly the female element personified in Clair. John and Henry are presently so little differentiated that they could be amalgamated without much loss. A lack of specificity like this means that characters are still in a rudimentary phase. But for an early outline that is quite normal.

What could we do to get more mileage from Paul's two protagonists? We could require them to have contrasting temperaments, histories, and needs. To see how this might work, imagine that John is married and always thinking about his wife and baby at home, while Henry is single and wanting to learn from John how one finds a mate. Later he is deeply attracted to the (unavailable?) Clair. Even complications as unremarkable as these endow the piece with far greater potential than at present, because they generate other issues and conflicts that are characteristic for these young men. They offer many opportunities for further scenes of tension and emotional exchange.

> *Developing the characters* means supplying each with a particular temperament, particular behavior, particular tastes and needs, and a particular background. In *plot-based drama*, the characters thoroughly fulfill the imperatives of the story line. In *character-based drama*, the story line emerges from the peculiarities and drives of the characters. No matter at which end of the spectrum you start, interesting characters and a good story are always symbiotic and will influence each other in the writing.

Now we'll go one a step farther and give the two not only differing circumstances but mismatched temperaments. This raises the stakes, by charging the space between them with useful *complications*. Let's make one man headstrong and the other slow and cautious. They may madden each other, but under different testing circumstances first one then the other temperament may be the more appropriate. This allows each to learn not only his own strengths and weaknesses but also to appreciate what it means to be different, and that there are different ways of tackling life's obstacles. Maturing—the point of this screenplay—may really turn out to be learning a flexible tolerance, an appreciation of those unlike oneself. It may also require arriving at a more settled idea of one's own

> *Complications* in a dramatic plot are the difficulties, obstacles, and distractions that characters need to encounter so their characteristics emerge under pressure. Most of what we learn in life, we learn the hard way, and this truth guides much fiction.

characteristics and limitations. Underlying the characters and their trajectory must be a value system, or philosophy of life.

When you develop the potential that flows from your characters' differences, your audience begins to look not just *at* them but *through* them, so they experience each of the characters' ways of seeing the other. We begin to see how John sees Henry and how Henry sees John. Instead of a neutral and omniscient view of the two young men, we come closer, experiencing each character as he experiences himself, and alternatively, as he or she perceives the other characters.

This lends the richness and complexity of real life without real life's prolixity. Since we're making art, not a simulacrum of life, the succession of counterpointed views must eventually be pared to something light, succinct, and swift moving. An Arthur Miller play in its first complete draft may be *eight hundred* pages long. Editing and compression reduce it to perhaps one hundred.

The important difference between a short film or short story and their longer brethren the feature film and novel is that the long form can develop a whole tapestry of characters and subplots. The preeminent creator of characters was Charles Dickens, and from reading his novels D. W. Griffith is said to have learned how to run several story lines concurrently, cross-cutting from one to another. This is called *parallel storytelling*, and it is useful for creating variety and pace. A *subplot* is an independent story line that will eventually intersect with one already existing. It may contrast with the main plot, complement it, or provide more action and complication.

In Paul's story, we are with John and Henry in every scene. Subplots could separate them and show them with other characters. There could be scenes involving only the subsidiary characters. For instance: Betsy Ross making her flag while

---

Subplots and parallel storytelling allow:

Digression. Situations, characters, and other issues can develop outside the main story line. We see the main characters in other relationships and thus see new sides to them.

Tension. The audience engages with characters and issues that may or may not become immediately germane. Subplots should always intersect with the main plot, but the audience wonders how and where this will happen.

Narrative compression. Cutting between several ongoing story lines allows each to be pared to essence.

Imagination. Multiple story lines imply complex patterns in life and invite the audience members to use their knowledge of life and their powers of interpretation or prediction.

Active participation. A complex story makes us an active participant rather than a passive receptacle for something easy.

Multiple POVs. Multiple story lines remind us that there are many viable points of view, many ways of being and doing.

the two young men are getting their orders; Clair saying goodbye to her husband; the announcement of his death; Clair's life after the young men have left to go onward; Washington's troops losing their flag, then carrying on, suffering and flagless; even of men taking their clothing apart to begin making something, which we later learn must have been their own flag.

This helps, but doesn't overcome, the concentration on the two main characters. Maybe this is the point; perhaps there should be no subplots. It is after all a road movie, and being continually on the road is what matters. Certainly, doing a lot of historical research would open a Pandora's box of possibilities, as well as enabling the writer to get the period, speech, and issues correct so that a historian could approve of the results.

In critiquing this first draft of an idea, which is already quite large, we could not go much farther than we have here. Paul would listen, make notes, and go away to ponder the ideas behind the suggestions. He would, if he were wise, not do anything for a few days, and then he would incorporate only those he strongly agreed with and found exciting.

MORE ON THE WRITING PROCESS

A writer can deal with only the topmost layer of problems in any draft. As an artist, one must also hold tenaciously to the integrity of the original idea. Otherwise, by acting precipitately after someone has reacted, one can lose one's own identity, which is disastrous. This, always a risk until the piece is finished and immutable, is probably why so many students only let people see finished work. Later they regret not being able fix flaws, which now exist in the locked-down, final print as huge, embarrassing deformities.

We have said that in making screen art there is no such thing as beginner's luck. You never win the jackpot by avoiding analysis, and you never get a hole in one, as you can do in golf. A film script, like a novel or an epic poem, is an evolutionary series of drafts. Each pass deals with the most major prob-

Writing is really about rewriting. Here are some tips about process.

1. In a new draft, don't try to fix everything.
2. Deal only with major problems until you get them right.
3. There will always be a subsidiary layer of problems to tackle.
4. Eventually your attention will fan out to the finest detail. At that point you will have to decide when to let go.
5. Return to your premise or working hypothesis frequently, to check whether your piece's center of gravity has shifted.
6. Keep earlier drafts. Perfectionism is uncomfortably close to obsessive compulsiveness. Sometimes writers are unable to avoid damaging their work.
7. If this happens, take comfort in knowing that you are truly dedicated.

lems, and each fix brings its own fresh prospects and introduces further problems. An artwork is like a tent. If you want your tent to look and function like a perfect tent, you cannot experiment with the length of one guy-rope without adjusting all the others.

By tackling questions and deficiencies, the film writer (with, most importantly, his or her artistic collaborators) is able to interrogate the piece and grope forward to an ever more complex and harmonious story structure. Even in outline form, where dialogue is at most summarized in a line or two, characters begin to manifest themselves powerfully. Since scene outlines usefully bar characters from speaking, it is by their individual actions, appearances, and differing agendas that they must establish themselves. This is a powerful avenue of development for the screen—or indeed, for any other kind of drama.

GOING FARTHER

There is an almost limitless amount published on writing the feature screenplay. Here are a few of the best-known texts. Develop your own work, define your own interests and needs before exposing yourself to this imperious, name-dropping crowd. Look before you buy, and make sure that tone and scope are to your taste.

Blacker, Irwin R. *The Elements of Screenwriting: A Guide for Film and Television Writing.* New York: Collier Macmillan, 1986.

Field, Syd. *Screenplay: The Foundations of Screenwriting.* New York: Dell, 1982.

Field, Syd. *The Screenwriter's Workbook.* New York: Dell, 1984.

Horton, Andrew. *Writing the Character-Centered Screenplay.* Berkeley, CA: University of California Press, 1994.

Hunter, Lew. *Lew Hunter's Screenwriting 434.* New York: Perigee, 1998.

Vale, Eugene. *The Technique of Film and TV Writing.* New York: Simon & Schuster, 1982.

For much debate and dialogue on screenwriting, not all of it elevating, try http://www.cyberfilmschool.com on the Internet, and use the links you find there to get to other, related sites.

PART IV

THE EMERGING WRITER

Revisiting Your Artistic Identity

Early in this course, you made a self-survey and from this a conjectural profile of your artistic identity. Since then, you have been writing furiously for weeks. Now, since you have a body of work from which to extract further information, the time has come to take stock. This time your conclusions will be less speculative, because you are assessing choices and responses you made during a series of creative endeavors. From choosing its own direction and solving a hundred problems, your creative self has unequivocally asserted itself and has made evident its own outlines. Now, in the peace after the battle, you can look back and discern the pulse and bearing that your creative self adopted during the fray. What you will discover this time should reveal a pattern based on a body of work rather than on surmise. Identifying any patterns will allow you to move forward with greater assurance.

ASSIGNMENT

1. Restate the two themes you originally thought you should work with (in the assignment for chapter 6).
2. Now list the themes that emerged in your writing. To remind you, the writing assignments were the following. Do you see common denominators?
   a. A tale from childhood
   b. Family story
   c. A myth, legend, or folktale revisited
   d. Dream story
   e. News story
   f. Adapting a short story
   g. A documentary subject
   h. Thirty-minute original fiction
   i. Feature film idea.

3. From the above notes, and any others that you may need, prepare a seven-minute class presentation outlining what you've discovered about your artistic identity. You can use these sentences as prompts or incorporate what they ask for in your own words:
   - "At the beginning I thought my *preferred themes* would be. . . ." [from (1) above].
   - "From the work I produced, my *dominant theme* was. . . ." [from (2) above]
   - "I see that I mostly want to *make my audience realize* that. . . ."
   - "I mostly want to *make my audience feel*. . . ."
   - "From writing in this class, I think *my vision of life is*. . . ."
   - "*I learned from working with the other writers* in this class that. . . ."
   - "*My next piece of writing* will probably be. . . ." (briefly describe topic, genre, any particulars).

CLASS DISCUSSION

After hearing what each class member has to say, here are some suggested topics for investigation, should discussion run dry (!):

- Do any common themes emerge from what class members said about themselves?
- During the course, what has emerged about the class and its processes?
- What is surprising or unexpected?
- Given the expectations at the beginning, what have people found harder than expected?
- What was easier than expected?
- Which stories stand out from everything you heard during the course?
- What in particular did you learn about using short forms?
- What was it like trying to work in long (feature) form?
- What new knowledge will you carry with you about the artistic process?
- Which people have formed teams for future work and what decided this?

YOUR OWN CREATIVE DIRECTION

In this book I have advocated not psychoanalyzing the creative self but simply acknowledging it and recognizing the kind of work it wants to do. This is the work you can only do with sustained passion, so it makes a lot of sense to know and cooperate with your own creative direction.

They say that truth liberates, and for most people the creative self will already be a half-familiar friend. For those who may be troubled about that, the creative self may seem like a dark force, which they prefer to avoid artic-ulating in public. If you feel this strongly, it cannot be wrong. Being more circumspect doesn't preclude you from work in the arts, however, since many a fully functional, working artist denies or suppresses the underlying forces in his or her psyche. So why (in the old country phrase) try to fix what ain't broke? Your instincts will tell you unerringly what course you should take—here and in all else.

WHERE TO GO WITH YOUR CREATIVE IDENTITY

From hearing what everyone in the class said about their creative identity, and from the discussion that followed, you now have ideas about yourself and where you stand in relation to the majority. You have made some public commitments about how you want to act on your future audience, and maybe what topics you think you should tackle. But where in fact *do* you go from here? What do you do with what you know, or think you know, about yourself?

From many years of observing those who accomplish their goals (and also, sadly, those who do not), I can say that most people make only vague plans for their future. They put themselves into school or into a job and then wait for the gods of chance to reveal the next step. A few are clear about what they want, and these folks nearly always seem to get there.

What do these people have in common? They like the work's process as much as the product. They first imagine the outcome into existence. Then they put their hearts and souls into building the shortest, strongest bridge that will get them to what they imagined.

Only a minority do this. Most people are fatalistic and avoid going in any defined direction, perhaps fearing that any focus will shut out other chances that may happen along. Instead they base their highest ambitions on what friends have done, and they put off setting any goals. When the time for studies runs out, they have to take whatever work, palatable or otherwise, they can find. It must be admitted that this fatalistic, passive approach some-times delivers, but seldom anything you would have chosen. A large part of my early career happened along these lines, but I think I was lucky. It's much better to figure out what you like and go for it with everything you've got. You are more likely to be good at it, and you are more likely to be chosen for it, *because* your passion shows. Everyone wants to employ, or work with, people who are passionate about what they do.

Let's set a few goals. The important part of your artistic identity is not *what* you are, because that can change. If you know you want to be a writer, what matters most is to know what stories you are equipped to tell and how to write them.

Avoid the obvious path, which is to take a thematic concern and write about it. Unless you are very skilled, this leads not to drama but to illus-trated morality lessons. Although the desire to teach everything one knows about life is initially very attractive, carrying it through soon becomes sterile and tiring. Even if you finish, your audience is likely to find the results too much like preaching.

Actually, you need not concern yourself about theme or meaning until you have written a draft or two. No matter what creative work you engage in, your underlying concerns will always surface, whether you want them to or not. Should something new come to light, you should, of course, be aware of it, because that means that you've moved on. But once your themes and authorial leanings are familiar, pay them no attention.

Let's look instead at the *way* that you will work, and you can decide from your own reactions how best to go forward. Here are some issues to ponder:

- Fulfilling the assignments made you step into a range of writing roles. Which most intrigued and energized you? Was it working with memoir, actuality, oral history, folk forms, or adaptation?
- Which, in contrast, did you find arduous and least energizing?
- Read through your writer's journal at a sitting. Next day, see what you remember. Which characters, places, objects, situations, actions, and themes are in the forefront of your memory? One's recall only holds what is special, so you can rely on it to winnow and refine effortlessly the work you should do. What do you find yourself contemplating?
- What is still scary to attempt? Anything one is scared of is something one needs to do—maybe now, maybe later, when one is more ready for it.
- How did you most like to get started? With a character, a situation, a myth, dream or legend, a dream, or an image? Which?
- What expertise has your life given you that others don't have? How did it come out in your writing work?
- What work do you think it's your responsibility to do, if you can contrive a way to do it?
- What genre or genres do you think are yours? Some people only want to work with documentary, fiction, mystery, or comedy. Which really calls to you?
- Which of your works got the best response from the class? What does this tell you?
- Among class members, who was closest to your values? Was the sense of kinship mutual? What kind of person is he or she, and what does that tell you about yourself? (Keep in mind that we are often attracted to, and need, someone different rather than similar.)
- Would that person be available as a writing partner?
- What kind of work would you want to do with that person? Have you approached him or her about it?

From looking frankly into all these aspects, try making writing a three- to five-year private agenda for the future. It can list classes and set out your own course of research and study, but most important is to work out what you intend to do, and a time frame to do it in. It must also culminate in something ambitious.

If you think of yourself as a writer/director, aim to write work for other people to direct, thereby establishing yourself as a versatile writer. If you begin by directing, try to direct good work written by someone else. You will have more distance on it and therefore more control. Concentrate as a director on becoming a good interpreter. If you direct your own writing and it's less than perfect, you won't know whether it's your directing or your writing that needs more work.

In your agenda, include researching how agents operate, how and when you should get one, and if there is something the entertainment industry needs that fits what you are really good at producing. Be bold in your plans but realistic about how long each work will take. Don't shoot yourself down through unrealistic expectations.

Try making up your three-to-five-year agenda with a plan for each project, like this:

Project Description	Dates	Stages	Preparatory Work per Stage
		1	
		2	
		3	
		4	
		5	
		6	

Column 1 contains the project description, column 2 the projected dates, column 3 the expected stages in producing the piece of work, and column 4 notes any preparatory work you will need for that stage. Write down everything you must do to get there, and make sure you set a practical path.

In your agenda, you may want to specify the reward you will accord yourself for accomplishing each project, especially if you stay on schedule. It's important to recompense yourself for good, consistent effort.

Don't talk to anyone about this plan, or you could talk yourself out of it. Reveal its existence as one of your rewards once you have accomplished your agenda's summit.

Now that you know where you are going, you can go to work on the first part of the first project. Should you modify the plan if you get behind?

Yes. Be ready to do whatever is necessary to keep moving along a planned route.

Make conferring with a mentor, or finding one, a part of your plan. Remember, most of what you will need to be a writer is a great hunger to understand life, as well as a willingness to write and write and write about what you see. For a writer, as my friend Lois Deacon once said, nothing that matters is real until one has written about it.

Good luck!

The next part of the book discusses how to expand any of your outlines into a screenplay. After that comes a section for teachers or facilitators on how to use this book in a course.

PART V

EXPANDING YOUR WORK INTO ITS FINAL FORM

Story-Editing Your Outline

If you know that your scene outline still has kinks, handcuff yourself to the nearest radiator to stop yourself from expanding it yet. People often imagine that moving to screenplay form will make problem solving easier, but architectural predicaments don't vanish because you start building the house; they get worse. First solve all the story difficulties in the story-editing phase.

This chapter deals with a range of dramaturgical problems and their solutions. Making the right adjustments will often bring wondrous changes. At this point it is really helpful to break the outline into movable parts by making scene cards (see sidebar, "Scene cards"). Scene cards let you try structural alternatives, which are still very much open when the piece is at the outline stage.

> *Scene cards.* Put each scene on its own numbered index card. This lets you line them up on a table and experiment with removing or combining scenes to judge the effect of changes. Being ready to do this is especially valuable during story conferences, when critics suggest alternative sequences. It quickly becomes apparent what works and what doesn't.

STRUCTURAL OPTIONS

When you review the structure of a given piece, any one of several determinants comes into play, depending on the priorities you choose. The differences between *linear* and *nonlinear* story lines are mostly distinctions in the handling of time, or in the working of the consciousness chosen to organize the story. I will go into this shortly.

Though nonlinear stories may seem attractively random, they are not really random at all. They just conform to a different logic. To begin seeing how all this might work in one of your own pieces, try applying the questions immediately below and pondering the possible answers.

1. How did I handle the story's basic time line? The initial answer categories are:
   Option 1: The story was told in chronological order.
   Option 2: It was told (or could be told) in some other order.
2. Whose POV predominates? Possible categories are:
   Option 1: A character in the story.
   Option 2: Multiple viewpoints from several characters.
   Option 3: That of the omniscient storyteller.

A linear story is easiest to follow, because it either follows chronological order or stays with a simple plot line. Telling a story chronologically implies that the events are being seen objectively or historically, from the outside.

A nonlinear story conveys more immediacy and subjectivity. It also demands more of its spectators, because they must decide what logic governs its progression. This might be purely an association between similar actions (cut from A wiping his brow to B wiping his car windshield), or a similar image (cut from car headlights approaching at night to the eyes of a hunting cat). Short films exploiting design or movement can easily sustain their formal structures using these kinds of linkage, but a longer piece can survive only by revealing a larger, enclosing design. Peter Greenaway's films are well worth seeing for the way they challenge most of the traditional notions about character and story structure. The *nouvelle vague* French novelists of the 1950s and '60s, such as Alain Robb-Grillet, Natalie Sarraute, and Michel Butor, made similarly bold experiments in changing the structure and texture of the novel.

Another less plotted approach is to structure a piece around the sensations of someone's experience. Under psychological pressure, a character hardly notices clock time or the actual order of events. For instance, a man who finds he is a victim of robbery does not chronologically revisit the events since he lost his belongings. His mind rushes to whatever is most important, and his body blindly carries out what his mind dictates. First he rifles his memory for the most likely moments when someone could have got into his briefcase. Provisionally he recalls three likely occasions. He reconstructs each occasion sketchily, in search of a quick and obvious answer. There being none, he goes into each occasion in detail, making and correcting memory errors, recalling "might-have-been" alternatives and trying comparisons between likely moments. Triumphantly he then recalls someone sitting nearby who turned away with a strange expression, then got up and abruptly left. He knows the man's name but not where he lives. . . .

The point is that emotion often affects how we travel through time, space, and memory. Emotion can block out much of the familiar world and create disorientation, or it can create an orientation along internally driven priorities. It may also extend time (boredom from waiting for a nonexistent bus) or compress it (suddenly a wallet gone, man running for doorway, hero yells "Stop thief!"—someone tackles thief but he breaks free. . . .).

When subjectivity is so dominant, the sequence and rhythm of events become important windows on the POV character's state of mind. In an action thriller like Andrew Davis's *The Fugitive* (1993), the torrent of action and reaction alone provides most of the insight into Dr. Richard Kimble's priorities, feelings, and vulnerabilities.

This shows, I hope, that point of view and the handling of time are inextricably entwined. Despite the apparent objectivity of the camera, a screen story is really a stream of consciousness. Point of view can originate in one character and migrate to another; ultimately, it can move around in this way with the mind (or collectivity of minds) behind the making of the film, which we can think of as the unseen storyteller.

There is more that influences structure. The subject itself may dictate aspects of the story's structure. If it has a complicated historical setup, it will be important to establish some of the characters, events, era, and backstory before the action proper can go forward. A story's structure can also be influenced by its genre. A story set in India might borrow from Indian dramatic repertoire and structure its story, by a succession of moods, not by Hollywood plot precepts at all. A surrealist story about a fireman who secretly sets fires might employ the apparently inconsequential shifts of place, character, mood, and scale characteristic of nightmare. A film about identical twins separated at birth might cut between serendipitous moments and events until they finally meet. A film about an archeologist might go chronologically backward, digging a metaphorical trench downward through layers of time, and coming to rest at some point of origin in his development.

A story can also mix antithetical narrative logics and thus alternate between moods and structures. In a tale about a baffled psychiatrist trying to help a soldier suffering hallucinations from post–traumatic shock syndrome, the narrative line might cut between two very different points of view. The doctor is in the present, while the patient has long interludes in which he relives past terrors or events that are imaginary or misremembered. Depending on whose POV we share, the language of the movie will shift back and forth radically.

We can say this: a story's structure need not be cast in the chronological mold of mainstream realism. It can arise from its mood and context, its association with similar stories, from the logic of its characters and from their psychology or mood. Film is a reproduction of consciousness, and everyone, all the time, is thinking and acting according to conjunctions of inner and outer imperatives. These may be in harmony, or they can be in conflict.

Whatever option you take, your structure must be one that your audience can understand is derived from the story's source with respect to character, narrative style, topic, genre, or message.

TROUBLESHOOTING

Here are a number of recommendations designed to flush out problem areas and provide solutions. Dealing with a script's problems is like having a wonderfully interesting and running dialogue with it. The script poses a problem (which you or someone else sees), and you come up with a solution. Putting it into effect has consequences elsewhere, as altering a single guy-rope does on the structure of a tent. Next you deal with other, maybe lesser problems—and you keep going until something or someone tells you it's time to stop.

Get us involved with the main characters quickly. Don't waste time working up an atmosphere, introducing us to the rugged landscape, and so on. A deliberately slow pace was all right for nineteenth-century readers with excess time on their hands, and it can still work with a captive audience in the theater, concert hall, or cinema. But most

> *A "contract" is implied whenever drama begins.* Clues planted for the audience suggest what the piece will deal with and how the piece will handle it. An effective contract (also called the "hook") lures the audience into the piece and holds them there.

screen drama will be seen on a domestic TV set, and your audience will click channels if your piece drags. Be bold. Claim your audience's attention with action that commits the characters to a compelling situation. This starts a momentum—something that Shakespeare (who had a whole company of actors to feed) knew very well. Consider how often his plays start in the middle of the action, in a whirlwind that leaves one gasping to catch up.

Let the audience know quickly what the piece will be about. Your tale is fatally handicapped if minutes roll past with no hint of its focus. It's like waiting and waiting in a restaurant where nobody thinks to give you a menu. Make a quick course of study to see how others begin their works: run the first minutes of a few feature films and note how soon and in what ways the most successful claim your attention. Do the same with the first two pages of

> *Foreshadowing* means literally to throw one's shadow ahead. In drama, it means using dramatic hints to prefigure an event and to set up tension in the audience. A dark musical theme might foreshadow the villain's appearance, and the sun emerging from behind clouds might symbolically foreshadow the heroine's recovery from a fever.

several novels. First prize surely goes to Tolstoy's *Anna Karenina:* "All happy families are alike, but each unhappy family is unhappy in its own way." Right away Tolstoy pops you in the face by proposing that happy families are boring and that the rest are made vital by their conflicts. You may not agree, but you surely read on.

Hide exposition. Every story has basic information—about the era, place, backstory, characters, relationships, people's agendas—that the audience needs to know at some time. Camouflage exposition by feeding it visually or by hiding it inside action. To realize we are being briefed by the author is like catching the puppeteer at work.

Double-check for vital expository information. It's fatally easy for the author, who already knows all this stuff, to leave out something vital. Guard against this by training yourself to read with a newcomer's lack of foreknowledge. This is a discipline all its own.

Keep exposition minimal, and space it out. When you ask your audience to absorb new situations or meet new characters, keep extraneous information till later to avoid informational overload. Avoid clumping expository information, or we will miss part of it. Make us wait till we need it, then hold each item back till we *really* need it. Some truly vital information may need reinforcement at different points if it is too subtle to absorb in one pass. In the final version you can always eliminate what proves unnecessary.

> *Scan each character.* As a useful exercise, try staying with each substantial character alone for the length of the piece. Write a subjective narrative of his/her needs, feelings, and perceptions— even when he or she is off screen. It will help you find and add what is missing. When flat characters become round, they stop being foils and add their own tensions and needs to each situation.

Whose story is it? You should often revisit the issue of whose story it is, what point of view should prevail, or whether you have chosen wisely. If this is a fundamental problem, you have not yet decided who or what the piece is about. Everyone at some point experiences this dilemma. One way to solve it is to experimentally privilege several points of view in turn, either throughout the piece or in particular scenes. Try rewriting the working hypothesis under these new conditions. This is fascinating if unsettling work.

Make them laugh, make them cry, but make them wait. Storytelling is like striptease. Disrobe too fast, and you've blown your act. Give us questions to answer, dilemmas to judge, and contradictions to weigh. Keep us guessing as long as possible so we exercise our minds and emotions, and stay in that wonderful state of anticipation.

Keep the story moving as new characters come on the scene. Don't stop the action so we can meet a new character. Action is rhythm, and in jazz you seldom silence the rhythm section to bring in a new soloist. On the contrary, the rhythm section often carries the newcomer.

Don't invent a new character to solve a plot problem. If she is indispensable, make her a functioning part of the story well before you make her perform that vital plot function.

Make sure the characters have enough opposing and contradictory qualities. Conflict is at the heart of all drama, so define your characters by their differences, making sure they have differing temperaments, backgrounds, habits, likes, dislikes, and agendas. This will plunge them into the pressurized situations between each other upon which drama depends. All interesting people have internal contradictions as well as external conflict. This indicates their unfinished business in life. Many people marry their opposites as part of their quests.

Know what your characters are trying to do or get. After deciding a character's dominant motivation, the inexperienced writer often fails to keep that character evolving. The most important question to keep asking during a rewrite is, "What is this character trying to get or do *now?*" You can devote a whole reading to querying each character's needs—minute to minute, hour to hour, day to day, or throughout his or her life. Keep searching for answers to this simple little question, and you will create characters who are questing and dynamic instead of passive and monolithic.

Raise the stakes, but keep them credible. Whatever stops each character from getting or doing what he or she desires can often be intensified. That makes the characters work harder and play for higher stakes. Drama about nice middle-class people leading materially comfortable lives may be flat, because one cannot credibly raise the stakes without introducing sensationalism. Make real life your teacher and decide what specifically creates unhappiness in real people's lives. Don't settle for a formula; get specific. Make some documentary films if you need to stay with ordinary people and penetrate to the drama in their lives.

Vary how you act on your audience, but maintain the intensity of demand. Beginners' work is often monotonous, because the scenes are too similar in type, rhythm, or content. Variety and contrast keep us fresh, which can be a strong argument for parallel storytelling. Another common fault is to make irrationally high or low demands on the audience's attention, sometimes overworking it by compressing or truncating a complex situation, and sometimes boring it with indulgent late-night discussions or artful montages about the coming of spring. Look at your piece with an imaginary "intensitometer" in hand, assessing each scene's demands on the audience.

Kill your darlings. Any scene, no matter how dear to the writer, is excess baggage if the piece works without it. The same is true for characters. Less is always more. Kill all conversation that can be rendered as action. Kill unnecessary characters. Get rid of everything that doesn't have a fully defined function in your dramatic mechanism.

See if the climaxes are well placed. A barometric chart for your whole story (see Fig 13–1, p. 125) will show where the high points lie in each scene and whether they are high enough. These are the climaxes, and one of them should be the turning point for the whole story. How well distributed are these high points? Are they bunched? Do they come too early in the story, leaving you with too much falling action? You can sometimes redistribute the high points by using the scene cards and transposing them. This may reveal that you are using the wrong point-of-view character, starting the story too early or too late, or taking too long to establish the characters' problems.

Check for multiple endings. How your story takes leave of its audience determines its final impact, since this is what the audience will remember. Chris Eyre's *Smoke Signals* (1998) is a lovely film, but it has no fewer than three endings. This is a common fault, and it muffles and confuses any story's most potent weapon, its parting shot. Multiple endings happen because the makers hang on to a multiplicity of messages. Look rigorously at your piece, identify its thematic backbone, and choose an ending that is appropriate.

Keep reworking your working hypothesis. As your piece evolves, its premise keeps altering. Updating it is hard work, but it will force you to revisit the core of your intentions, which may have evolved far more than you think. You must know fully what you are doing—and let it be said loud and clear that most people do not. Remaking the hypothesis is also the surest way to define the appropriate ending.

Put your work away for a few days before rereading it. Distance alone can help you see what everyone else can see. Partial blindness from overfamiliarity is an occupational hazard.

18

Dramatic Conventions

If you acted on the recommendations in the last chapter, you probably had the queasy feeling that your tale is being taken over by outside forces. You are right. But they are nothing that I have invented. They are the dramatic conventions, forces that bear no less powerfully on everything a person writes than does the pull of the moon on the oceans. So before we can look at expanding an outline, we should see why dramatic conventions possess such invasive authority.

Knowingly or otherwise, every writer operates in adversarial intimacy with the bloodlines of their art form. I, for example, am working to make adequate use of the English language as I write this book, because to do otherwise would risk losing the attention of you, my good and faithful reader. Languages are agreements about meaning, agreements that have taken much of man's history to evolve. The conventions particular to drama and poetry are just as functional and have probably been around for nearly as long. They survive and prosper because they facilitate our drive to exchange narratives. Any writer, actor, dancer, songwriter, or comedian who enthralls us has made it their business to master those conventions. Film is so inextricably joined to its sister arts that many of its methods of presentation simply extend and amplify the more ancient visual and linguistic forms of discourse.

Structural forms and genres are part of the same cultural tool kit. When we recognize a familiar structure or genre, it triggers particular expectations. The conventions of the mystery tale, for instance, set up audience anticipations that are quite different from those of romantic comedy. So a genre, like a language, is a set of accepted norms that exist to ease communication, not imprison it.

None of the conventions are immutable, however, since storytellers often splice together genres or types of discourse and playfully subvert the audience's expectations. In that way conventions, like spoken language, continue to evolve and remain lively.

A story told to an audience is like a bridge being constructed from both sides at once. On one side the teller signals what he intends to build toward the audience. Beginning to spin the tale, the teller discharges interests, concerns, or inner pressures that he or she thinks are interesting to the audience. The audience on its part suspends disbelief and builds its end of the bridge, as heightened receptivity. If the relationship proves sustaining, the audience will work really hard—mentally and emotionally—to meet the teller halfway and keep their side of the pact.

But delivering a tale poses a conundrum for the teller. If she concentrates overmuch on second-guessing her audience, she may lose the very core of herself, the source of her tale's authenticity and of her own "voice." Conversely, should she ignore common ground and focus inwardly on personal concerns, she may instead use references too personal for others to recognize or care about.

Between these extremes lies a noble and practical ideal—that stories of depth can be of personal concern and yet touch others unlike us, bridging the existential void between us.

The skillful teller of tales enters our mind as if it were his or her own house and tells the tale so it invokes a mental and emotional dialogue in us. However, we are not empty vessels waiting passively to be filled. We very much want to be active participants. By connecting actively we work our way out of isolation. Audiences and creators are thus united by a common and unacknowledged purpose—to replace the stalking desolation of existence with a discovery of "what is," together uncovering some of life's hidden meanings.

You must already know what this feels like, since you have had the heady experience in class of sensing an electric current running through everyone. Somebody says or writes something very special, and the class practically shivers, then goes still and silent. At that moment, all are one. What a feeling!

Now we can tackle expanding an outline into a fuller work.

GOING FARTHER

Roemer, Michael. *Telling Stories: Postmodernism and the Invalidation of Traditional Narrative.* Lanham, MD: Rowman and Littlefield, 1995. (Michael Roemer's excellent and challenging book is about the historical, philosophical, and psychoanalytic underpinnings of storytelling. It covers antiquity to postmodernism, beginning with the unsettling assertion that "every story is over before it begins." Erudite and scholarly rather than prescriptive, it is written nonetheless in highly accessible language and will send you back to examine every assumption you ever made about narrative. The author convincingly maintains that story is ultimately an aspect of ritual in which humankind equips itself to handle destiny. Roemer, himself an accomplished filmmaker, is professor of film and American studies at Yale University.)

---------19---------

Expanding Your Outline

Let's presume that you have gone through multiple outline drafts and that your work has been critiqued by several candid and demanding readers. By this time, your story line should be well developed, and you justifiably feel ready to expand it into a screenplay, stage play, or a literary form. The guidelines that follow may seem rather sketchy, but there are good reasons for this. Guidance toward full expansion is rather beyond the scope of this book, but also I believe that too much preparation would be counterproductive. It is important to try one's hand first and generate problems that one wants to solve. It is at that point that extensive resources become helpful.

Here are some tips to get you started. With each is a short bibliography to point you toward more specialized help—if and when you need it.

SCREENPLAY FORM

Turning an outline into a screenplay mostly takes a sense of what makes good cinema. It is the aesthetic, not technological, side that you need to master. Though any received truth always has its exceptions, I would say that good cinema:

- Has crucial differences from other art forms, such as dance, music, literature, theater, and painting but partakes of them all.
- Makes use of the collaborative process by assigning a lot of the final creation to director, actors, and technicians. Trust these people, and do not try to take control of what they do.
- Selects subjects, characters, and settings for their cinematic appeal. Go *with* cinema's grain, not against it.
- Exploits actuality by using real situations and locations whenever possible rather than trying to recreate them. Cinema has to be based on the concrete, because the camera and microphone must always

181

have something actual to record. This is all the more true for low-budget cinema.

- Tells a story by visual rather than verbal means and so is best when it dwells on action, reaction, and behavior rather than conversation.
- When it uses dialogue, reproduces the feel of natural conversation by using its essence, not its bulk.
- Excels in revealing the subjective states of both characters and storyteller.
- Makes use of sound's emotional associations and narrative possibility.
- Avoids overinforming us, by leaving as much as possible to the audience's imagination. A bar where two characters meet can be evoked by just a few key details and the right background atmosphere.
- Makes good use of the audience's inculcated knowledge and expectations. These are the conventions mentioned above. They are always in need of refreshment by original minds. Every living language is in continual change.

STANDARD SCREENPLAY FORMAT

The industry screenplay standard has evolved as the ultimate in convenience to all concerned, so do not invent your own. The specimen page in Figure 19–1 shows the standard format, which conveniently yields around a minute of screen time per page.

Scene Heading. Each scene begins with a flush-left, capitalized scene heading that lists:

- Scene number (Don't bother numbering scenes until all rewrites are complete, since it creates confusion when you are still splicing different drafts together)
- Interior or exterior
- Location description
- Time of day or night.

Body Copy. Scene or action description, mood setting, stage directions. Double spaced, away from scene headings and dialogue, and running the width of the page. Body copy (sometimes called *stage directions*) should:

- Use minimal but colorful language.
- Stipulate nothing irrelevant or impractical.
- Set a scene impressionistically, never comprehensively ("Unmade single bed, ashtray full, underwear overflowing from drawers, crucifix hanging crookedly" is brief and tells us plenty).
- Give action descriptions that leave room for interpretation ("Brad looks around nervously," not "Brad puts his right-hand index finger

41. EXT.—SUBWAY STATION—EVENING

Subway station in poor part of town, garbage blowing on sidewalk. KATIE, early 30s, stocky build, labors along carrying a heavy shopping bag. At sound of APPROACHING TRAIN, she breaks into an awkward run.

> KATIE
> (to herself)
> Damn and damn again. . . .

42. EXT.—SUBWAY PLATFORM—EVENING

Katie clatters down the steps on to platform and looks up the line to the approaching train. A hand touches her shoulder. She whirls around in defensive alarm, then her expression changes to wonderment.

> KATIE
> You're already here! How did you get here so fast? You frightened me, creeping up like that.

VADIM, early 40s, dark clothing and greying beard, smiles at her quizzically. He takes the shopping bag, looks inside, and tears open a packet of crackers, offers her one, which she takes.

> VADIM
> (chewing)
> They don't know I'm here yet?

> KATIE
> Of course not! This time it's your call, not mine.

Vadim opens his coat and pulls a yellow, snake-like ferret from an inner pocket. He wraps the animal around his neck like a muffler and dusts his nose with its tail. Katie draws back. She is afraid of all animals. Vadim is more amused than ever.

> KATIE
> It smells! I can smell it from here! What is it anyway?

Vadim goes to give it to her, but she quickly retreats.

Figure 19–1   Standard Screenplay Format

on his lower lip and inches forward to see around the gloomy, gray-painted stairway." Overwriting fatally clogs the reading process and alienates actors, director, art director, and camera crew, by trying to do their jobs for them).

- Boldly, briefly, and evocatively set a mood. ("Raw dawn over wet, lackluster streets" fires the reader's imagination and challenges the cinematographer in just the right way).

Character Names.   Names appearing outside dialogue are in all-capitals in screenplays only when they first appear. In TV script form and stage play layout, the convention is to capitalize all names to help actors quickly find their parts or stage directions and to signal which characters populate each scene.

Dialogue Sections.   Dialogue sections are:
- Headed by the speaker's name, capitalized and centered.
- Block indented.
- Preceded and followed by a space.
- Accompanied, when strictly necessary, by stage directions inside brackets.

Good Screen Dialogue
- Is brief and compressed, because art lies in essence, not quantity.
- Has the flavor and rhythm of each speaker.
- Should be a verbal action—that is, trying to act on or elicit something from other characters.
- Has strong subtext. Characters in films, like people in life, seldom say directly what they really feel or want but instead betray it in other ways.
- Never duplicates what the audience can see, as in, "That's a smartly cut brown tweed coat you're wearing."

Camera and Editing Directions
- Are a distraction, so don't use them. To a professional, it's unprofessional.
- Transitions like "Cut to," "Dissolve to," are capitalized and used *only* when indispensable to sense. Place consistently either flush left or flush right.

Sound and Music Directions
- Specify sounds (in capitals) only when they strongly advance the mood or narrative ("Heavy FOOTSTEPS approach the other side of the door").
- Don't specify type or placing of music unless it has special meaning to the viewer.

Notice that the screenplay sample in Figure 19–1 gives no camera or editing directions. It is true that industry practices vary and that some commercial scripts are hybrid creatures, trying to dramatize their contents by looking like a shooting script. This may help to sell the script in a particular quarter, but even from the hands of a seasoned professional, it has little practical value to the director. Play safe, force yourself to write minimally, and let specialized readers interpret with their own creativity.

Actually, the screenplay format is a trap, since its appearance and proportions suggest that films are built around dialogue. This may be true for TV work, because watching TV is not a primarily visual activity. Good screen drama is not verbal but visual and behavioral. To see how little appears in a good screenplay, examine the original screenplay for a film you admire. Be careful what you read, since much that is published is release scripts— transcriptions of finished films, not the all-important starting documents.

One way to circumvent the anxieties of staying in correct format is to use screenwriting software, such as the very popular Final Draft, which automatically formats screenplays, TV episodes, and stage plays. It has a variety of excellent features, including a spell checker, thesaurus, and an index-card and outlining feature that takes the agony out of wholesale rewriting. Check out the latest version's features at on the Web, at http://www.finaldraft.com. Many software companies offer discounts for educators and registered students.

On writing from a screenwriter's perspective, there is a profusion of texts. Below are some useful ones, but try to browse in your local bookstore until you see one that calls to you. You can also find texts of all kinds through Amazon, or Barnes and Noble, two vast and well signposted Internet bookstores (http://www.amazon.com and http://www.barnesandnoble.com. Both systems make it easy for you to find related books or books by the same authors.

Going Farther

Dancyger, Ken, and Jeff Rush. *Alternative Scriptwriting: Writing beyond the Rules.* Boston: Focal Press, 1995. (Deals with alternative and experimental forms but offers a succinct approach to mainstream ones, too. Exercises, case studies, personal scriptwriting, and non-Hollywood work.)

Egri, Lajos. *The Art of Dramatic Writing.* New York: Simon & Schuster, 1977. (A classic text that is still influential. Very strong on dramatic construction.)

Field, Syd. *Four Screenplays: Studies in the American Screenplay.* New York: Dell, 1994. (Analytical script dissection of four potboilers, *Thelma and Louise, Terminator 2: Judgement Day, The Silence of the Lambs,* and *Dances with Wolves.* Shows how the scripts function, includes interviews with writers.)

Field, Syd. *Screenplay: The Foundations of Screenwriting.* New York: Dell, 1982. (A punchily written favorite, with much good advice on stylistic and structural aspects. Useful to those wanting to succeed in classic Hollywood terms but may seem over formulaic and alienating to others. Chillingly revealing about what producers look for.)

Field, Syd. *The Screenwriter's Workbook.* New York: Dell, 1984. (Exercises and step-by-step instruction. Same caveat.)

Lumet, Sidney. *Making Movies.* New York: Vintage, 1996. (Though not specifically about screenwriting, this more than any other account of recent years conveys lucidly and modestly what making feature films is really like.)

Rabiger, Michael. *Directing: Film Techniques and Aesthetics,* 2d ed. Boston: Focal Press, 1997. (This is a complete manual for film directors, with a strong emphasis on their authorial responsibilities. See in particular Part III ["Writing and Story Development"], Part IV ["Aesthetics and Authorship"], and Part V ["Preproduction"]. These will give you a good idea of how a director works with a screenplay and how he or she develops a performance in collaboration with script and actors.)

Hills, Rust. *Writing in General and the Short Story in Particular.* Boston: Houghton Mifflin, 1977, revised 1987. (Although not about writing for the screen, it is extremely helpful in developing short-form narratives. Exceptionally well written and full of good, practical advice and analysis. A large proportion of my copy is underlined.)

Seger, Linda. *Making a Good Script Great,* 2d ed. Hollywood, CA: Samuel French, 1994. (Good and practical.)

Vail, Eugene. *The Technique of Screen and TV Writing.* New York: Simon and Schuster, 1982. (A coolly classic text that compares what is fundamental to film, theater, and literary forms. Has a pleasant intellectual distance.)

For an online library of finished screenplay work in search of an agent, try the following Internet sites, extensively described in an excellent article by Bonnie Rothman Morris in a *New York Times* article of 14 January 1999, page D7:

Allworld Screenplays, http://www.mynox.com/writers.htm, where scripts are listed by genre.

Spec Screenplay, http://www.hollywoodlitsales.com, which has both buyer and seller postings.

A.D.I. Feature Entertainment, http://www.adifentertainment. thefilmstudio.com, where an unfunded independent filmmaker solicits scripts.

Drew's Script-O-Rama, http://www.script-o-rama.com, which reserves a section for scripts looking for buyers. This site has links to over six hundred TV and feature scripts, some of famous films.

American Zoetrope, http://www.zoetrope.com, is Francis Ford Coppola's site, which invites submissions under a workshop plan. Those submitting must first critique four other people's scripts.

STAGE PLAY

Writing well for the stage means knowing what works best in the theater. Learn all you can about the medium's production processes, because it will influence how you think and work. The limitations of the live stage are obvious: parallel storytelling, montage, or altering time are difficult, because they require elaborate scene building and a lot of scene and lighting changes. These changes are expensive and intrusive; they require great professionalism if they are to work.

Since most of a theater audience is some distance from the players, dialogue, action, and body language tell more than what passes over a character's face, which is often remote or even hidden from large sections of the audience. The theater's strength is that it is a live, three-dimensional medium and perfect for projecting us into the dynamics of relationship. Sustained dialogue scenes, frowned upon in modern cinema, are the norm in stage plays. Another strength is that space in the theater is fluid, because it can be abstract. One set can function, with a few different props at each change, as many different locations.

The page layout for a stage play script (see Figure 19–2) is dense and compressed, because actors often carry the whole script in one hand during rehearsals. While film is rehearsed and shot in fragments, plays evolve from actors and director doing extensive interpretive and developmental work "from the book." Only after thoroughly exploring interpretations is it safe to learn lines, since a wrong meaning becomes internalized once lines are committed to memory.

ACT II

Megan and Art's apartment at night. Poorly furnished, rickety furniture, with a doorway leading into the bedroom. MEGAN, who is pregnant, is trying to follow some sewing directions at the old fashioned treadle sewing machine. ART, who seems to have just got up, enters from the bedroom, putting on his outdoor jacket. Seeing her look at him, he gives her a perfunctory kiss.

ART.   Hi babe. Don't wait up. I'm going to Blackie's to see Tommy.
MEGAN.   You're going out? You said you were going to stay home more. . . .
ART.   Didn't know Tommy was going to be in town.
MEGAN.   You said you weren't going to stay out so much. You *said* so.
ART.   But this is Tommy.
MEGAN.   So?
ART.   Best friend from the Detroit days (MEGAN is silent). You know, *Tommy.*
MEGAN.   But we said we'd see your mom.
ART.   Gotta be another day. Tommy called up when you were asleep.
MEGAN.   That's the second time you've skipped out on your mom.
ART.   Oh boy. Will ya quit naggin'? I'll call her from the bar.
MEGAN.   Artie, your mother is very sick.
ART.   I know she's sick. Think I'm stupid? I know she's sick. . . .
MEGAN.   Art, she's got cancer.

Figure 19–2   Standard Layout for Stage Play

Writing for the stage requires that you use each character and setting to the maximum. Having a few characters meet in a common space, such as a kitchen, garage, garden, or hotel lobby, is good, because in such settings people can come and go in different combinations. Every communal space is a potential pressure cooker for human relationships, but a play will become prohibitively expensive if you specify too many characters and settings. By focusing deep and avoiding realism, a play can work wonderfully well in a minimalist setting—*Waiting for Godot* can be mounted in a black space with three garbage cans and some stools. Because theater can set up an atmosphere of abstraction, a play can handle metaphysical contemplation much more directly than can a film.

It is truly fascinating to see how many ways the theater has functioned for its audiences throughout its history. Read up its history and go see as much theater as you can afford. Make notes of your impressions and ideas.

Large cities usually have developmental groups who stage readings of new work and give writers feedback and critical discussion. This is a good place to learn from observing. If you put your own work on the block, force yourself to listen carefully and nonjudgmentally; at all costs, avoid going into defensive explanations. This is a harrowing but ultimately liberating rite of passage.

As for screenwriting books, search in libraries, bookstores, or online stores to find what will personally suit you. See the earlier mention of Final Draft writer's software, which handles stage play formatting as well as that for cinema and TV.

Going Farther

Cassady, Marshall. *Characters in Action: Playwriting the Easy Way.* Colorado Springs, CO: Meriwether, 1995.

Catron, Louis E. *The Elements of Playwriting.* New York: Macmillan, 1994.

Egri, Lajos. *The Art of Dramatic Writing.* New York: Simon & Schuster, 1946, 1972.

George, Kathleen E. *Playwriting: The First Workshop.* Boston: Butterworth-Heinemann, 1993.

Hatcher, Jeffrey. *The Art & Craft of Playwriting.* Cincinnati, OH: Story Press, 1996.

McCusker, Paul. *Playwriting: A Study in Choices and Challenges.* Kansas City, MO: Lillenas, 1995.

McLaughlin, Buzz. *The Playwright's Process: Learning the Craft from Today's Leading Dramatists.* New York: Backstage Books, 1997.

Packard, William. *The Art of the Playwright: Creating the Magic of Theatre,* New York: Paragon House, 1987.

Pike, Frank, and Thomas G. Dunn. *The Playwright's Handbook.* New York: Penguin, 1996.

Sweet, Jeffrey. *The Dramatist's Toolkit: The Craft of the Working Playwright.* Portsmouth, NH: Heinemann, 1993.

Van Itallie, Jean-Claude. *The Playwright's Workbook.* New York: Applause Theater Books, 1997.

Wright, Michael. *Playwriting in Process: Thinking and Working Theatrically.* Portsmouth, NH: Heinemann, 1997.

MAINLY TEACHERS

For Class Leaders

This book is designed principally for college or university–level media classes, but it can be tackled alone, or informally by friends or associates in a self-help group. This chapter discusses methods, ideas, and purposes to help anyone new to leading an ideation writing class. It also deals with responding to the work submitted, class size, organizing, and scheduling.

Why is ideation needed in schools? There one finds the next generation. Anyone who sees much of the beginner's fiction that emerges from film schools or from aspiring independent filmmakers might suspect an international plot to brainwash the young into making the same ideas over and again. (Documentaries are a little healthier. Perhaps because many are located in contemporary life, they are usually fresher and more interesting.)

Why is so much fiction so unimaginative? Here are some possible causes, factors that reach beyond the ubiquity of television:

- The homogenous age and social class of most film students.
- Film education is a new discipline, whose teachers still have much to learn and many problems to solve.
- Most film schools are only two or three decades old and have had to concentrate on getting production up to decent standards.
- Most film students set out to become a writer/director and assume that they only need to acquire proficiency in production to become one.
- Finding a good idea and writing a good script is a need that only shows up when the student is a senior—gaining control of the medium but also running out of time.
- Most novice writers are in the dark about the creative process's origin in the self, and few writing programs tackle ideation as distinct from screenwriting.
- Screenwriting manuals mostly assume that good ideas come automatically to the talented. They don't. They have to be uncovered through specialized work.

- Though scripts are written and discussed by the thousand in every film school, they are usually critiqued only after the basic idea has been set. By then, the omelet is difficult to unscramble.
- The enemy of fresh and cinematic ideas is the screenplay format itself. Being a theatrical sketch for the screen, it encourages the user to imagine that cinema is mostly dialogue.
- Student writers compound their problems by hiding their ideas so they won't get stolen.
- Screenwriters of all degrees of experience often cannot define their screenplays' premises.

Any attempt to critique a work requires the critic to uncover its central purpose. This is hard, but the outcome of this process regularly amazes the writer. To me, this suggests that a stage of consciousness raising is being regularly overlooked prior to turning ideas into screenplays. That's what this book sets out to address.

WHERE DOES THIS COURSE BELONG IN A CURRICULUM?

This course can go anywhere in a full media syllabus, from at the beginning to somewhere midway. Because classes I taught were electives, those taking it were usually intermediate or senior film students who already liked writing. A round of outcome assessment applied to some core production classes at Columbia College Chicago showed definitively that students were mastering film techniques far better than they were communicating with their audiences. The faculty decided to make Idea Development (as we call the class) the portal of entry to the entire film school.

Though a camera assistant has less need to understand story essentials than a director or screenwriter, we felt that everyone benefits from an ideation workout. Making stories is, after all, the entire point of making films at all, and it should not remain foreign to anyone educated in a film school, no matter which craft they end up pursuing.

So far we have found that, with some modifications, the class has functioned extremely well as a gate of entry to the first hands-on production classes. Since most students were freshmen, the culminating projects had to be simpler than they had been for those more senior, and they had to aim more consciously at the visualization that students needed in their upcoming Film Techniques I. We do find that a substantial proportion of the students, facing a class that requires them to define ideas, grumble at what they take to be a remedial or therapeutic activity. But by the end of the class, virtually all are converts. They know a lot more about the artistic process, and they can see the value of their work. Subsequent screenwriting classes can now start at a higher level of sophistication.

To summarize: class assignments and methods need to be adjusted according to the students' level, sophistication, biases, and expectations of the medium. Some variations we have already tried will be discussed later in this chapter, and we expect to start a Website in which your experiments and ours can be made public. Please look for it in the Film/Video Department's area of Columbia's Website, http://www.colum.edu.

CLASS SIZE AND DURATION

Although Columbia College Chicago is an open-admissions college, with what we believe is the largest film/video department anywhere, we make sixteen students the maximum class size. I have taught up to eighteen elsewhere, but such large classes make it difficult to give everyone's writing sufficient classroom attention. Toward the end of the course, the teacher also risks being engulfed by reading and marking if the class is too big. Although initial projects are brief and in outline, the later projects tend to be dense and to call for prolonged analysis.

Classes can also be too small. A class of fewer than six or eight may lack sufficient momentum, especially if the class is required rather than voluntary. Teachers always depend on the enthusiasts to help provide momentum. When this energy is missing from a small class, the teacher has to supply it, and this makes for incredibly uphill work.

The discussion about scheduling later in this chapter reflects the fact that the course was designed for a regular, fifteen-week college semester, but since the work is modular, you can easily adapt it to other lengths. (See "For Courses Longer or Shorter Than Fifteen Weeks," toward the end of this chapter).

At Columbia our classes meet once a week for three hours, but two meetings a week are better, if space and teacher availability permit. It takes three to four hours of weekly meetings to do justice to four or five people's work, but the classes are intense, and in long sessions fatigue sets in during the third hour for both students and teacher. Two two-hour sessions would be ideal.

SCHEDULING

In the appendix there is a model syllabus for a standard fifteen-week course. This can easily be modified according to taste and experience. Later in this chapter there are suggestions for doing this, including alternative assignments useful for different kinds of students.

MARKING THE WORK IN PREPARATION FOR CLASS READINGS

Goals and objectives for the assignments are stated in each chapter, but with experience you may want to start putting your own in your syllabus.

If I can, I mark the work immediately before class meetings, so it is still fresh in my mind. To keep the workload from overwhelming me, I set up a template reply in my computer and fill in the blanks for each student. One template sentence, for instance, assesses how successfully the writer has kept to the outline form—beginners habitually drift into the past tense. Another criterion assesses how the characters have emerged or the tale is structured. These criteria are developed from the goals and discussion topics. To these generic assessments I then add some lines of individual commentary, plus the all-important grade.

This course favors continuous assessment (as opposed to the approach that sets just one or two knowledge exams per semester). Students can see how they are doing and get feedback on which of their skills needs work, from the first assignment onward. My grading tends to be encouraging at first, then more critical as students develop standards for the work they are doing.

By arranging everyone's work in grade order and looking at my records to see whose work is due for exposure, I choose which assignments to read out next in class. Because everyone seems to write at least one or two outstanding pieces, this seems to work.

From the chosen projects I also note the teaching points I can make. Also, I can raise the class's awareness with respect to certain aspects at the start of the class.

RUNNING CLASS SESSIONS

Set up chairs in a circle, or better, around a couple of large folding tables, so that everyone can see everyone else. Initial class sessions focus on games and small-group improvisation work. Groups can break out and huddle in the corners.

Playful activities at the outset break the ice for those new to each other. Play also encourages class members to take chances and trust their spur-of-the-moment instincts, since the stakes are not high at this point. Initially you will need to give class members every encouragement to speak freely and put their feelings and instincts out before the group. Help this to happen by speaking freely from the heart yourself whenever the occasion allows. At first it will be difficult for the more inhibited to follow your example, but most come to love the adrenaline that courses through the class as people open up with their ideas and responses.

Have your class play the Instant Story Game (or anything like it) sporadically throughout the course if you can, using the class bank of students' index cards and pictures. It is especially useful as a refresher when students show signs of fatigue from too much analysis or discussion. Something fast, intuitive, and spontaneous can revive flagging energies and remind everyone how brilliantly inventive they are under pressure.

The chance to have their work read in class (not to mention the need for a passing grade) motivates most students to keep up with the deadlines.

According to the maturity and work habits of your students, you may need to penalize late work explicitly, since the class cannot function if the majority of its members do not hand work in on time.

After the first few classes, reading the best four or five pieces for presentation and critical discussion takes up most of the classroom time. Because writers reading their own work aloud often gabble, in modesty and confusion, one gets better results if one designates the person sitting next to the writer to give the reading. If a writer reads his or her own work there is also diminished contact with the audience, since the reader is self-conscious and focused on the act of speaking. But being a listener during the presentation allows writers to experience how their works act on their first audiences. This firmly extracts writing from the ghetto of therapeutic personal expression and places it as a performance in the public arena. Writers mentally compare their work's effect with what they had imagined, and when right in the public eye they often make major discoveries. This is sometimes touchingly visible and palpable for everyone.

Some of the activities have time limits, and in the interests of giving equal exposure it always matters that presentations and critiques stay within reasonable limits. When I have a session coming up where I know I am likely to be distracted from timekeeping or am going to have difficulty cutting people off, I bring a little cooking timer that beeps after a preset countdown. Students understand the value of being able to deliver in a set time, especially those who already know how important "pitching" ideas has become for writers, directors, and producers trying to elicit funding.

Collaborative disciplines like film or theater require exceptional relationships between their co-creators, so working on ideas as a class can lay some truly portentous foundations. Most important is that class members learn how to diplomatically use critical and analytical concepts, how to pursue the creative process, and how to give and take criticism.

The teacher's personality is a fundamental catalyst in this process. You will be the role model who demonstrates how a critic approaches another person's work. Doing it with respect, searching out the core of the writer's intentions, and respectfully contributing constructive ideas for change are transferable skills that students learn by example. Under your guidance, the class should always seek to further what the writer has started, not competitively to dismantle and rewrite it. Strongly encourage comments describing what the speaker felt, saw, or realized while the piece was being read, and tactfully redirect students who instead center on whether they liked or disliked it. The least helpful critic is the person who insists on saying how much better he or she would have handled the idea. This is appropriation, not constructive criticism. It is best deflected by explaining how desirable the positive approaches are by comparison. Once the class grasps these principles, it will spontaneously protect its members from wrong treatment.

When a writer has been successful, the audience feedback—verbal or nonverbal—will offer palpable evidence of the fact. By treating everything as a work in progress, one can always be encouraging and demonstrate where the areas of next development lie. This promotes hope and enthusiasm. It is most moving and gratifying to see the expression of naked wonderment on a writer's face when the class finds patterns and ideas that go beyond what the writer had consciously realized. These moments—and they're not rare—are ones you will specially cherish. They send waves of awe through the class.

A class with good morale will develop strong sympathies and an atmosphere of kindly humor. Your curiosity, warmth, humor, and supportiveness will do much to create this, and you will have the high satisfaction of seeing like-minded people teaming up together and forming partnerships for future projects.

FOR COURSES LONGER OR SHORTER THAN FIFTEEN WEEKS

To make the course shorter and fit into the quarter system of ten weeks, I suggest dropping the Adaptation project, either the News or the Documentary project (but not both), and the Feature project. Given the time available in any normal-length course, the latter is usually done so incompletely that its main value lies in helping beginners understand how massive an undertaking it is to write a feature.

To make the course longer, consider having your writers do a myth, a legend, *and* a folktale instead of choosing one from the three options. These are enormously rewarding sources and really should not be compressed into a single assignment. Also valuable would be more than one example of the Childhood, Family Story, and Dream projects, as these are normally very strong and personal. More time could be allotted to some later projects, such as the Thirty-Minute Fiction Film and the Feature projects. Simply reading and analyzing more projects in class will usefully slow progress through the projects.

ALTERNATIVE METHODS AND INFLUENCES

To make a design and to share it means giving it away for development, and I am happy to say this is already happening. Our Screenwriting Center runs over fifty sections of Idea Development annually, so new ideas and new configurations are constantly on trial. The design depends less on the goals than on the needs of the students and the methods and experience of the many instructors now teaching it.

I have always found the Tale from Childhood assignment very successful, but one teacher, Cassandra Mogusar, working with very young freshmen had less luck. Cassandra instead asked the class to map out their childhood neighborhood. The result was "a wonderful energy in the classroom as students drew their maps and recalled the quirky neighbor around the cul de sac, the park where everyone hung out, and the corner store."

Doreen Bartoni, who teaches both graduate and undergrad writing, finds that students need to do a sense-perception exercise the first day of the class. This can be drawn from any of the acting-school standard repertoire. It might involve:

- Being blindfold and exploring the textures in the room.
- Handling objects from a box and relating their associations.
- Being randomly turned on the spot and stopped, then relating in detail what one's eye falls upon.

Doreen and other teachers find that paying this attention to the actual "allows students to be in the world with open eyes, ears, nose, hands, and heart." She goes on to say:

> An artist needs to dance with the world of phenomena. Otherwise she'll have a tendency to live within the comfort of her cocoon. This exercise gave students a sense of discovery and awe. Another by-product was a sense of trust. No one was afraid of being made a fool of—the teacher included.
>
> As film is a visual medium, I would propose more visual storytelling. Perhaps the CLOSAT cards could be arranged in a storyboard fashion. I have brought in comic books to begin a discussion on shot size and editing. Also, I have used a very simple and direct exercise from Betty Edwards's *Drawing on the Artist Within* (New York: Simon & Schuster, 1987), which demonstrates not only the conventions of symbols but also shows a student's particular style. I also brought my students to the Art Institute and had them create stories from various pieces of artwork. The Art Institute idea comes from Cari Callis.
>
> An improvisation exercise could be useful. Perhaps one student could start a story and each student would add a line. Improvisation as well as your outlined group exercises helps to underscore the collaborative process of filmmaking. . . . I gave my students the option of bringing in sound clips or a sound track design to illustrate their dreams. This exercise provides an opportunity for students to connect with the power of sound to evoke moods and/or states of mind. Joe Steiff and I first used this exercise in the Image and Symbols class [a class in visualization].
>
> Finally, I think all of these assignments are fruitful and keep the students working hard. In a semester class situation I would allow for some breathing room. Perhaps lose the Feature Film assignment (which we have done in Idea Development) and build in a mid-term review.

Cari Callis comments:

> One of the most powerful things that has ever occurred in
> the classroom is when I asked each student to arrange their
> photos on the blank walls with stickem. I just stepped back
> and allowed them to create a collage. Afterward, as a group
> we explored each collage and looked for visual patterns, the-
> matic patterns in the photos and eventually deepened our
> discussion to discern patterns in the student's choice of
> arrangement. Some students overlapped images, created
> huge spaces, or were very linear or chaotic. We discussed
> how this arrangement affected our insight into the images
> themselves and made connections to how film does this
> through juxtaposition and editing.
>
> As well as working in groups I've also asked them to
> work in pairs. Students can then exchange cards and create
> stories. Sometimes I ask them to keep their own characters
> and choose a first reader's situation or act or theme. Also I
> ask them to exchange portfolios and answer a specific set of
> questions designed to make them think more deeply about
> each other's work. This also helps me greatly to find insight
> that I may have overlooked.

Joe Steiff, director of the Screenwriting Center, writes:

> We make the [Short Fiction] assignment into several short
> treatments/proposals (two 5 minute silent and two 5 minute
> sound film ideas) and replace the Feature assignment with
> a 15–30 minute longer assignment. In addition, we've added
> an assignment in which students draw or photograph a
> storyboard (shot for shot) of one of their 5 minute ideas.
>
> In preparing students to work in a visual medium, it helps
> to stress visualization in the assignments, especially when
> some students feel they are being held away from the hard-
> ware in order to make them do "more creative writing."
> However, one always walks a fine line. To accede too much
> to students' hunger for the medium can lead away from con-
> centrating on the act of mental visualization. I am always
> afraid that assumptions about the medium will take over
> unless the spotlight remains on ideas and storytelling. Dick
> Ross, of the National Film and Television School in England,
> places such a large emphasis on the role of the storyteller
> that he runs a class in which he and his students do nothing
> but tell stories. He believes that, like actors, students find
> the necessary confidence in exploring their own experience
> and imagination this way.

PARTING THOUGHTS

The storyteller is a figure revered in antiquity. It is no exaggeration to say that a civilization stands or falls on its storytellers' wit, daring, insight, and humane vision. They are the guardians of its values, wisdom, humor, and history. Nowhere are their talents more influential than in today's cinema. In tomorrow's cinema this may be truer still. For when inexpensive, high-definition videorecording and projection become the norm, production and distribution costs will fall and regional filmmaking will have a chance to prove itself, as regional theater has everywhere done in the last thirty years.

But for filmmaking to leave Hollywood and the few other international production centers, we shall need many excellent directors and writers. Where writers apprentice themselves, how they are to sharpen their discrimination, how they are to reach deeper into their abilities, is still an open question.

If better writing is to happen, there needs to be less attention to industry norms, more radical thinking, more involvement by writers with other artists and their aspirations, and much more attention to the pulse and fever of actual life. When writers respond to these challenges, production teams and actors' ensembles have no barriers to what they can give.

Teachers and students all learn from each other. This is very much a shared venture. May you derive as much pleasure and learning from your students and their work as I have from mine. May we all do something toward making a slightly better world.

APPENDIX: SCHEDULING A CLASS

Here is a skeletal syllabus for a standard, fifteen-week college semester. The notes on the first couple of pages lay out the goals and expectations, for those considering the course and for people who have enrolled but have no prior knowledge of what is entailed. Students should read the "Study Text" sections before each meeting. Many assignments require either prior research or development time, so the syllabus often calls for early reading of later chapters, to be reread just prior to the meeting at which they will be discussed. Students should feel free to read any part of the book ahead of the requirements. To save labor for instructors, we expect to put the skeleton syllabus on Columbia College's Website, http://www.colum.edu, and also on that of Focal Press, http://www.focalpress.com.

STORY IDEA DEVELOPMENT: NOTES AND SCHEDULE

Instructor: _____
Office Address: _____
Contacts (Phone, email etc): _____
Course Number: _____
Meeting times: _____
Building & Room #: _____

Text: Rabiger, Michael. *Developing Story Ideas.* Boston: Focal Press, 2000.

Goals
- Understand and value some of the experience that has formed you.
- Approach the creative process in a variety of ways.
- Draw on a variety of sources that are personal, cultural, or observational.

- Articulate your own artistic identity and review it in the light of further work.
- Create screen fiction ideas in outline or form.
- Create some screenwork ideas based on actuality, which nevertheless serve as vehicles to communicate your own thematic concerns to an audience.
- Learn the fundamentals of dramatic tools and criteria.
- Use dramatic criteria as tools to make screen ideas evolve.
- Work with others collaboratively instead of competitively.
- Give and take constructive critique.

Your Development: You will be required to write to the deadlines and then submit your work to the critique of your audience. You will need to:

- Write every week. (No work is accepted more than a week late.)
- Use a word processor and its spell checker, or a typewriter. (No hand-written work is accepted.)
- Attend every class, and on time.
- Expand, modify, and redefine your artistic identity at the end of the semester.

Attendance Policy: Attendance is mandatory if students are not to get fatally out of step.

Grades: Written critical feedback and a grade is given for each assignment. The final grade for the course is based on:

- Average of grades accomplished for individual assignments.
- Energy and consistency of effort.
- Contribution to class discussions.
- Amount and quality of work accomplished during the semester.
- Attendance.

Resources: You will need what is listed below as you progress through the semester. Start now. Making records and squirreling away what might come in handy is a writerly habit.

1. *Writer's Notebook.* Keep a small notebook with you at all times and jot down descriptions or sketches of what you see around you. Tag each entry in the margin with one of the six "CLOSAT" codings, thus:
     C = description of a *Character* who could be used in a story.
     L = interesting and visual *Location.*
     O = curious or evocative *Object.*
     S = loaded or revealing *Situation.*
     A = unusual or revealing *Act.*
     T = any *Theme* that intrigues you or that you see embodied in life.

2. *Dream Journal.* This is entirely private, kept at home and used for the Dream Sequence assignment. Keep a record of your dreams here.
3. *News File.* Save good news stories in a folder for use in the News Story and Documentary assignments. Go through old magazines and papers; you'll find noncurrent material that no one else is using.
4. *Picture File.* Save pictures from magazines and newspapers. Strong inspiration can come from your choice of a war photograph, crime report, fashion ad, or a landscape.
5. *Instant Story Cards.* On certain weeks (see the schedule), hand in your best observations as index cards. With them we will play a game of Instant Story. No handwritten cards are acceptable, so make cards *on standard five-by-eight-inch format, and typed*, as below. You can staple or gum computer print to the index cards.

Your initials	Descriptive tag	Code letter
P.P.R.	*Ronnie, Movie Theater Manager*	C

Seventyish man with shock-white hair combed back in a sweep to cover his bald spot. Dressed in cheap suit pants and shirtsleeves, heavy wire-rim aviator glasses protecting his sliver eyes. Swears like a sailor at the staff of the crumbling movie palace, and laments the bygone days of Hollywood and black-and-white. Greets any patron over sixty-five with a smile, scowls at all others. Smokes and sucks on coffee incessantly.

SAMPLE SYLLABUS FOR STORY IDEA DEVELOPMENT CLASS

Text: Rabiger, Michael. *Developing Story Ideas.* Boston: Focal Press, 2000.

Week 1

Class: Course overview; divide into working groups; class discusses and develops its own criteria for good ideas and good critical feedback. Start your journal of dreams and observations. Describe importance of dream journal and collecting CLOSAT materials (Characters, Locations, Objects, Situations, Acts, Themes, as well as news stories, pictures).

Study Text: Chapters 1, 2, and 3 for next session; chapter 6 to work toward the Artistic Identity assignment due Week 4.

Week 2

Due: Chapter 5, CLOSAT assignment (six Instant Story index cards, two each for Characters, Locations, Objects).

Class: Play Instant Story, then develop criteria for interesting story elements (CLOSAT—Characters, Locations, Objects, Situations, Acts, Themes). How to observe and develop characters, how to define and develop situations. Metaphoric thinking.

Study Text: Chapters 4, 5 for next session; Chapter 12 to begin searching for your ideal short story for the Adapting a Short Story assignment due Week 9.

Week 3

Due: Chapter 5, CLOSAT assignment (six Instant Story index cards, two each for Situations, Acts, Themes; also six Instant Story pictures, two each for Characters, Locations, and Objects). Remember to write your initials and the appropriate ID code on your picture contributions, too.

Class: Discuss the part of time and place in stories (weather, time, location, mood). Point of view. Analysis versus Intuition. Play Instant Story game using CLOSAT cards and images.

Study Text: Reread Chapter 6 for next session; Chapter 9 so you can start a search for your ideal Myth, Legend, or Folkstory to adapt to a modern setting, due Week 7.

Week 4

Due: Chapter 6, Artistic Identity assignment.

Class: Relationship between content, form, and style. Structure, symbol, roles, advocacy, life's imprint. Play Instant Story game using CLOSAT cards or images.

Study Text: Chapter 7 for next session; Chapter 10 to prepare for Dream Story assignment due Week 8.

Week 5

Due: Chapter 7, Tale from Childhood assignment.

Class: Read aloud and discuss class members' Artistic Identity assignments. Discuss approaches and methods in selecting ideas for screen journalism. Play Instant Story game using CLOSAT cards or images.

Study Text: Chapter 8 for next session; Chapter 12 so you can start searching for material for the News Story assignment due Week 10.

Week 6

Due: Chapter 8, Family Story assignment.

Class: Myths as a bank of recurring human experience. Workshop. Read aloud and discuss class members' Tales from Childhood. Dreams—their meaning and creative application.

Study Text: Reread Chapter 9 for next session; read Chapter 11 so you can start researching material for the Documentary Subject assignment due Week 11.

Week 7

Due: Chapter 9, Myth/Legend/Folkstory Retold assignment.

Class: Read aloud and discuss class members' Family Stories. How to find good short stories; criteria for successful adaptations.

Study Text: Reread Chapter 10 for next session; read ahead Chapter 15 so you can prepare a sketch of the Feature Film idea due next week.

Week 8

Due: Rough sketch for Feature Film Idea due in preparation for Week 13 assignment; Chapter 10, Dream Story assignment.

Class: Read aloud and discuss class members' Myth/Legend/Folkstory Retold.

Study Text: Reread Chapter 11 for next session; read Chapter 14 so you start searching for material for your Thirty-minute Original Fiction assignment due Week 12.

Week 9

Due: Chapter 11, Adapting a Short Story assignment.

Class: Read aloud and discuss class members' Dream Stories.

Study Text: Reread Chapter 12 for next session.

Week 10

Due: Chapter 12, News Story assignment.

Class: Read aloud and discuss class members' Short Story adaptations. Structuring the feature idea and capitalizing on previous work.

Study Text: Reread Chapter 13 for next session.

Week 11

Due: Chapter 13, Documentary Subject assignment.

Class: Requirements of the short fiction form. Read aloud and discuss class members' News Stories.

Study Text: Reread Chapter 14 for next session.

Week 12

Due: Chapter 14, Thirty-Minute Original Fiction assignment (single subjective point of view).

Class: Read aloud and discuss class members' Documentary subjects.

Study Text: Reread Chapter 15 for next session.

Week 13

Due: Chapter 15, Feature Film Idea assignment (two points of view).

Class: Read aloud and discuss class members' Thirty-Minute Original Fiction ideas.

Study Text: Read Chapter 16 for next session.

Week 14

Due: Chapter 16, Revisiting Your Artistic Identity Assignment, with your total portfolio in a ring binder.

Class: Read aloud and discuss class members' Feature Film ideas. Review principles and resolutions emerging from course.

Study Text: Read Chapters 17, 18, and 19 for next session.

Week 15

Class: Read aloud or discuss in overview remaining Feature Film ideas. Discuss any issues arising from Chapters 17, 18, 19. Review principles and resolutions emerging from course.

Celebrate!

Index